Phyllis Finnie

Chinese Cooking
with Lucy Lo

Chinese Cooking
with Lucy Lo

Authentic mouth-watering recipes
you can prepare at home
by a leading
Hong Kong chef.

Horwitz Publications

Bucks Books

Published by agreement with
Universal Copyright Company (1959)

Published in Hong Kong 1979 by
Horwitz Publications
a division of Horwitz Group Books Pty Limited
(Hong Kong Branch),
Prince's Building, 8th Floor, Hong Kong,
a wholly Australian owned publishing company.
Australian address: 506 Miller Street, Cammeray, 2062

Distributed by Horwitz Group Books Pty Ltd,
506 Miller Street, Cammeray, 2062 and
Gordon & Gotch (A/sia) Ltd,
114 William Street, Melbourne, 3000, Australia

Copyright © 1979 by Lucy Lo
National Library of Australia Card No.
and ISBN 0 7255 0545 1

Printed in Hong Kong by Dai Nippon

*Recommended price only

Introduction

For centuries Chinese cooking as an extension of Chinese culture has developed a distinctive and unique style which is all the more interesting for its great variety. There are indeed hundreds of traditional Chinese dishes from different regional cuisines and the ones selected for this book are my personal favourites.

Chinese cooking is a living art which calls for the exercise of creativity, harmony, contrast, and ingenuity. Ingredients which are not easily available in the Western world can be substituted by others and in my recipes, I have duly indicated whenever suitable substitutes can be used.

Successful Chinese cooking is the result of understanding, careful preparation, technique, and inventiveness. One must approach Chinese food with the understanding that the Chinese regard food as something much more than just to satisfy hunger. It is true that food is life, a symbol of good things, good health, strength, and comfort. And so, cooking is highly pleasurable and the centre of family and social activities.

Preparation of the ingredients is of great importance. Many dishes require very fine chopping, subtle and correct seasoning, a matter of both technique and creativity. For instance, it is necessary to know how to use a Chinese cleaver for cutting and chopping. The fist should be closed and the hand is used to push the food towards the blade. Western kitchen utensils can be employed, but it is adviseable to use the traditional Chinese wok, the all-purpose cooking instrument for quick and versatile cooking. Stir frying requires good temperature control—the wok should be heated, then the temperature reduced before adding oil because if the wok is too hot, the oil will burn. The heat should be raised progressively for the addition of the other ingredients—slightly for onions and shallots, and then again for meat and other vegetables. The whole process may take no more than 5 to 10 minutes. Remember, NEVER OVERCOOK as this will destroy the flavour and the freshness of the food.

There are six basic flavours in Chinese food: sweet, sour, hot, spicy, pungent, and salty. Their distribution, proportion, and employment must be balanced and controlled for proper blending. Flavouring in Chinese cooking is applied at different stages, namely, the marinade for the seasoning of the principle ingredient (whether meat, fish, or vegetable); the seasoning of supplementary materials; the flavouring ingredients to vary the taste of food (such as black beans); sauces—the most important of which is soy sauce even though others such as oyster and plum, are often used. It is usual to add light soy for stir frying and dark soy for braising and stewing, and finally, table condiments and sauces as dips to add to the flavour of cooked food.

You should not ignore the garnish for a well prepared Chinese dish should appeal to the eye as well as the palate. A sprinkling of parsley, a slice of carved radish or cucumber can add a necessary dash of colour. The execution of exquisitely carved garnishing elements is a fine art itself in the Chinese kitchen.

Chinese cooking is a pleasure and a challenge at the same time. In closing, let me wish you many hours of experimenting and creativity, and above all, many enjoyable meals.

Lucy Lo

Contents

Poultry

雞, 鵝, 鴨.

Poultry is frequently served as the main course at a Chinese banquet.

It is customary to serve the whole bird and a number of recipes

for this have been included in this section.

It is also customary to serve the dish

with the head pointing towards the guest of honour.

To ensure that the flavour is retained throughout cooking

always select young birds if possible.

CHICKEN AND WALNUT
合桃雞丁

Ingredients

Chicken fillet, cut into cubes	10 ozs.
Walnut	4 ozs.
Bamboo shoots, cut into cubes	2 ozs.
Green and red pepper, cut into cubes	1 oz.
Carrots (cubed)	2 ozs.
Onion, cut into cubes	2 ozs.
Garlic, chopped	$\frac{1}{2}$ teaspoon
Ginger (shredded)	1 piece

Seasoning
(for chicken)

Light soy sauce	1 tablespoon
Cornstarch	1 tablespoon
Salt	1 teaspoon
Sesame oil	$\frac{1}{4}$ teaspoon
Sugar	$\frac{1}{2}$ teaspoon
Pepper	$\frac{1}{4}$ teaspoon

Oil	1 tablespoon
Water	1 tablespoon

Sauce

Water	2 tablespoons
Sesame oil	$\frac{1}{4}$ teaspoon
Cornstarch	1 teaspoon
Monosodium Glutamate	$\frac{1}{2}$ teaspoon

PROCEDURE

1. Cook walnuts in boiling water for 2 minutes. Drain and let dry, then deep fry until golden brown.
2. Mix seasoning ingredients to-gether. Roll chicken pieces in seasoning until well covered.
3. Heat 2 tablespoons oil, fry onions, peppers, ginger and bamboo cubes and put on plate.
4. Heat 3 tablespoons oil, brown garlic, and fry chicken and spring onions. Add sauce, mix well with walnuts and serve. Garnish with parsley.

Servings: Four to Five

SPECIAL BLACK BEAN CHICKEN
豆豉雞

Ingredients

Chicken fillet or drum stick, boned	12–16 ozs.
Black bean (preserved), mixed with 2 tablespoons oil, 1 tablespoon sugar and steamed for 3 minutes	4 tablespoons
Red chilli	$\frac{1}{2}$ tablespoon
Green chilli	2 ozs.
Garlic, chopped	1 tablespoon
Carrots (sliced)	4 or 5 pieces
Root ginger, shredded	2 pieces
Spring onion, sliced	4 stalks
Oyster sauce, 2–3 tablespoons	
Dark soy sauce	3 tablespoons

Seasoning

Light soy sauce	2 tablespoons
Wine	1 tablespoon
Salt	1 teaspoon
Sugar	1 teaspoon
Ginger juice	1 teaspoon
Pepper	$\frac{1}{2}$ teaspoon
Monosodium glutamate	1 teaspoon
Cornstarch	1 tablespoon

Sauce

Oyster sauce	2 tablespoons
Sugar	1 tablespoon
Wine	1 tablespoon

PROCEDURE

1. Dry chicken with a towel and cut into $1\frac{1}{2}''$ cubes.
2. Season with the above seasoning and allow to soak for 15 minutes.
3. Heat 4 cups of oil and quick fry chicken until it is more than half cooked. Drain.
4. Heat 2 tablespoons oil and brown garlic, ginger, onions and mix together with chicken, adding preserved black beans, stir fry chicken until it is almost cooked.
5. Add the above sauce, mix with green and red chillies and fry for 1 minute, ready to serve.

Servings: Four to Six

Top: Cooking Utensils

Below: Walnut with Chicken

Overpage Top: Special Black Bean Chicken

Overpage Bottom: Beggar's Chicken

Overpage right: Crispy Chicken

GINGER CHICKEN WITH HONEY SAUCE
蜜糖子羗雞

Ingredients

1 Chicken, chopped into bite size pieces	$2\frac{1}{2}$ lb.
Young root ginger, sliced	4 ozs.
Honey	3 tablespoons
Spring onion	2 stalks
Oil for deep frying	

Seasoning

Light soy sauce	1 tablespoon
Salt	1 teaspoon
Cornstarch	1 tablespoon
Sugar	1 teaspoon
Dark soy sauce	$\frac{1}{4}$ teaspoon
Pepper	$\frac{1}{4}$ teaspoon

Sauce

Honey	3 tablespoons
Cornstarch	1 teaspoon
Water	$\frac{1}{4}$ cup

PROCEDURE

1. Mix seasoning ingredients to-gether. Cover chopped chicken with the seasoning and quick deep fry for 3 minutes in oil. Drain.
2. Heat 2 tablespoons oil, brown ginger and spring onions. Fry chicken until well cooked. Then pour in honey sauce and a dash of light soy sauce and cook for another 1 minute.
3. To serve, garnish with parsley and pineapple.

Servings: Six

CHICKEN WITH PINEAPPLE SAUCE
生菓雞球

Ingredients

Chicken fillet, cut into cubes	$1\frac{1}{2}$ lbs.
Pineapple, chopped	$\frac{1}{2}$ tin
Melon, cut into cubes	6 ozs.
Lychee (drained)	1 tin
Shallot, chopped	1 tablespoon
Spring onion (sectioned)	2 stalks

Seasoning

Light soy sauce	2 tablespoons
Cornstarch	1 tablespoon
Sesame oil	$\frac{1}{2}$ teaspoon
Water	1 tablespoon
Oil	1 tablespoon
Salt	1 teaspoon

Sauce

Water	$\frac{1}{2}$ cup
Dark soy sauce	1 teaspoon
Salt to taste	
Shallot	1 tablespoon
Cornstarch	$\frac{1}{2}$ teaspoon

PROCEDURE

1. Marinate chicken cubes in the seasoning. Let stand for 10 minutes.
2. Heat 2 tablespoons oil, brown spring onions and shallots. Fry chicken cubes. Add chopped friuty pineapple and sauce and bring to boil.
3. To serve, place pieces of melon and lychees around the chicken.

Servings: Six to Eight

CHESTNUT WITH CHICKEN CUBES
栗子雞球

Ingredients

Chicken breasts, cubed	10 ozs.
Chestnuts, skinned and cooked	6 ozs.
Onions	4 ozs.
Shallots	2 stalks
Mushroom, quarters	4 pieces

Seasoning

Light soy sauce	2 tablespoons
Cornstarch	1 tablespoon
Sesame oil	$\frac{1}{2}$ teaspoon
Sugar	1 teaspoon
Salt	1 teaspoon
Water	1 tablespoon
Oil	1 tablespoon

Sauce

Oyster sauce	3 tablespoons
Sugar	2 tablespoons
Water	$\frac{3}{4}$ cup
Sesame oil	$\frac{1}{2}$ teaspoon
Wine	1 tablespoon
Cornstarch	1 tablespoon

PROCEDURE

1. Mix seasoning ingredients to-gether. Roll chicken pieces in seasoning until well covered.
2. Cook chestnuts in boiling water until soft.
3. Heat 3 tablespoons oil, stir fry onions, mushrooms and chicken. Add chestnuts and sauce. Cook to-gether for 1 minute and serve. Lettuce can be added at the bottom of the pot.

◄ Fried Duck with Onion Sauce

STEAMED CHICKEN
臘腸蒸雞

Ingredients
1 Chicken, cut into 20 pieces	2–2½ lbs.
Mushroom, soaked, cut into quarters	6 pieces
Shallots, chopped	2 stalks
Root ginger	2 pieces
Vegetable oil, warmed	4 tablespoons

Seasoning
(*For mushrooms*)
*Wine	1 tablespoon
Sugar	½ teaspoon

Seasoning
(*For chicken*)
Light soy sauce	2 tablespoons
Salt	½ tablespoon
Sesame oil	½ teaspoon
Cornstarch	1½ tablespoons
Pepper	¼ teaspoon
Sugar	½ teaspoon
Oil, warmed	2 tablespoons
Water	2 tablespoons

PROCEDURE
1. Marinate chicken in the seasoning. Let stand for 15 minutes.
2. Add seasoned mushrooms, ginger and spring onions. Mix well and place on a deep plate.
3. Steam chicken over boiling water for 25 minutes. Add 2 tablespoons oil, sesame oil and pepper before serving.

Servings: Five to Six
*See glossary.

BRAISED CHICKEN WITH BEAN SAUCE
碧綠柱侯雞

Ingredients
One chicken	2½–3 lbs.
Mustard Green, or seasonal vegetable	1¼ lbs.
Shallots, chopped	1 teaspoon
Garlic, chopped	1 teaspoon
Root Ginger	1 piece
Spring onion	1 stalk

Seasoning
Dark soy sauce	1 tablespoon
Wine	1 tablespoon
Root Ginger	1 piece
Spring onion	1 stalk
Salt	1 teaspoon

Sauce
Soy bean paste	3 tablespoons
Water	2 cups
Chicken cube, or monosodium glutamate, 1 teaspoon	
Dark soy sauce	½ tablespoon
Sugar	2 tablespoons
Wine	2 tablespoons
Cornstarch (Use later)	1 tablespoon

PROCEDURE
1. Dry chicken with a towel and season skin of chicken with dark soy sauce. Then, season inside of chicken with the rest of the above ingredients for 10 minsutes.
2. Heat 3 tablespoons of boiling oil in a pot or skillet. Add shallots and garlic. Fry chicken on all sides until a little golden brown, then add bean paste, stirring a little. Add sauce and braise chicken for 25 to 30 minsutes.
3. Remove chicken from pot, brush with sesame oil. Chop chicken into pieces and arrange on a plate. Thicken sauce with cornstarch and pour on top of chicken.
4. Heat 5 cups boiled water adding 2 tablespoons oil, 1 tablespoon salt and a pinch of cooking soda. Cook mustard greens (or other seasonal vegetable) in this for 3–4 minutes. Then arrange on both sides of chicken, ready to serve.

Servings: Four to Six

ORANGE CHICKEN
香橙燒雞

Ingredients
1 fat chicken	3 lbs.
Sliced oranges, for garnishing, juice and peel for cooking	2

Seasoning
Dark soy sauce	1 tablespoon
Pepper	1 teaspoon
Salt	1½ teaspoons

PROCEDURE
1. Clean chicken and rub dry. Rub with salt, pepper and soy sauce.
2. Put grated orange peel and 3 tablespoons orange juice inside of chicken.
3. Put chicken over a rack in oven and roast at high temperature for 40 minutes, turning chicken after roasting for 25 minutes.
4. Chop into pieces and serve, garnished with slices of orange and parsley.

Servings: Four to Five

SHREDDED CHICKEN WITH CELERY
芹菜雞柳

Ingredients

Chicken fillet, shredded	6–8 ozs.
Celery	4 ozs.
Carrots, shredded	2 ozs.
Mushroom, shredded	2 pieces
Shallots	2 cloves

Seasoning

Light soy sauce	1 tablespoon
Cornstarch	1 tablespoon
Sesame oil	$\frac{1}{4}$ teaspoon
Pepper	$\frac{1}{4}$ teaspoon
Sugar	$\frac{1}{4}$ teaspoon
Salt	1 teaspoon
Oil	1 tablespoon
Water	1 tablespoon
Ginger juice	1 tablespoon

Sauce

Water	3 tablespoons
Light soy sauce	1 tablespoon
Dark soy sauce	1 tablespoon
Sesame oil	$\frac{1}{4}$ teaspoon
Cornstarch	$\frac{1}{2}$ tablespoon
Chicken cube $\frac{1}{2}$, chopped, or $\frac{1}{2}$ teaspoon monosodium glutamate	

PROCEDURE

1. Heat 1 tablespoon oil and stir fry carrots and celery together with a pinch of salt, stirring well.
2. Season shredded chicken with the above seasoning and let it soak for 10 minutes.
3. Heat 2 cups of oil and quick fry mushrooms and chicken fillet for 2 minutes. Drain and put on plate.
4. Clean wok, then heat 1 tablespoon, oil. Brown shallots and stir fry chicken again. Add sauce, mix well with celery and carrots. To serve, garnish with parsley.
Fried rice noodles can also be added.

Servings: Four to Six

SPECIAL SOY SAUCE CHICKEN
豉油雞

Ingredients

One chicken	$2\frac{1}{2}$–3 lbs.
Root ginger	2 pieces
Spring onion	2 stalks
Parsley	$\frac{1}{2}$ oz.

Sauce

Light soy sauce	1 cup
Dark soy sauce	$\frac{1}{2}$ cup
Water	$1\frac{1}{2}$ cup
Wine	1 tablespoon
Sugar	$\frac{1}{2}$ cup
Chicken cube, chopped or	1 cube
Monosodium glutamate	1 teaspoon
Ginger	2 pieces
Spring onion	2 stalks
Aniseed	2 cloves

PROCEDURE

1. Clean chicken, blanch in boiling water for 1 minute and rub dry. Insert ginger and spring onions inside the chicken.
2. Bring sauce to boil and put chicken in. Cook for about 25–30 minutes. Remove from pot and let cool.
3. Brush chicken with sesame oil and chop into pieces, ready to serve. Garnish with parsley.

Variation: Hard boiled egg cooked in spicy sauce can be added.

Servings: Four to Six

CHICKEN IN WINE
醉雞

Ingredients

Chicken	2 lbs.
Leek or spring onions	2 stalks
Root ginger	2 slices

Seasoning

Salt	$1\frac{1}{2}$ teaspoons
Ginger juice	1 tablespoon
Wine	2 tablespoons

Sauce

*Hua Tiao, or Sherry	4 cups
Light soy sauce	2 tablespoons

PROCEDURE

1. Clean chicken and rub with salt. Place ginger and leek inside and steam for 30 minutes.
2. Soak chicken over night with wine and soy sauce.
3. Chop chicken into pieces and serve cold. Shredded jellyfish or shredded cucumber can be served as an accompaniment.

Servings: Four to Five
*Chinese Wine see glossary.

CHICKEN IN LOTUS LEAF
荷葉蒸滑雞

Ingredients

Chicken fillet	12 ozs.
Mushroom, soaked sliced	4 pieces
Bamboo shoot, sliced	2 ozs.
Spring onion, sliced or scallions	4 stalks
*Lotus leaf, fresh or dry	2 pieces

Seasoning

Light soy sauce	2 tablespoons
Cornstarch	1 tablespoon
Sesame oil	$\frac{1}{2}$ teaspoon
Salt	1 teaspoon
Sugar	$\frac{1}{2}$ teaspoon
Pepper	$\frac{1}{4}$ teaspoon
Water	$\frac{1}{2}$ tablespoon
Oil	1 tablespoon

PROCEDURE

1. Cut chicken fillet into cubes, and season with the above seasoning together with the other ingredients.
2. Soak lotus leaf in boiling water for 1 minute, drain and wrap all the ingredients into a parcel. Steam over boiling water for 25 minutes.
3. Open parcel with scissors and cut diagonally, add a little heated oil and spring onions, ready to serve.

Servings: Six
*Obtainable at Chinese grocer.

SLICED CHICKEN QUICK-FRIED WITH CAULIFLOWER
椰菜雞片

Ingredients

Chicken breast, thinly sliced	6 ozs.
Cauliflower	10 ozs.
Shallots, chopped	2 stalks
Garlic, chopped	1 teaspoon
Root ginger (shredded)	1 piece
Oil, for cooking	

Seasoning

Light soy sauce	1 tablespoon
Cornstarch	$\frac{1}{2}$ tablespoon
Sesame oil	$\frac{1}{4}$ teaspoon
Pepper	$\frac{1}{5}$ teaspoon
Sugar	$\frac{1}{5}$ teaspoon
Salt	$\frac{1}{5}$ teaspoon
Oil	$\frac{1}{2}$ tablespoon
Water	$\frac{1}{2}$ tablespoon

Sauce

Water, or broth from cauliflower	4 tablespoons
Cornstarch	1 teaspoon
Sesame oil	4 drops
Soy sauce	$\frac{1}{2}$ teaspoon

PROCEDURE

1. Marinate chicken with the seasoning. Let stand for 10 minutes, and put aside.
2. Heat 1 tablespoon oil, brown garlic, fry cauliflower, add $\frac{1}{2}$ cup water (or broth) and cook for 5 minutes. Add 1 teaspoon salt, drain, then remove to a plate.
3. Heat 2 tablespoons oil, brown spring onions, fry chicken slices until colour changes to white. Add sauce, mix well, pour on top of cauliflower, and serve.

Servings: Four

WALNUT WITH CHICKEN SLICES
合桃雞片

Ingredients

Chicken fillet, sliced	1 lb.
Walnut, chopped	4 ozs.
Cucumber, for garnish	4 ozs.
Tomato for garnish	4 ozs.
Oil for deep frying	

Seasoning

Salt	1 teaspoon
Sesame oil	$\frac{1}{2}$ teaspoon
Cornstarch	1 tablespoon
Light soy sauce	1 tablespoon
Sugar	$\frac{1}{2}$ teaspoon

Batter

Flour	1 cup
Cornstarch	4 tablespoons
Baking soda	$1\frac{1}{2}$ teaspoons
Oil	1 tablespoon
Water, enough to make batter runny	7 ozs.
Salt	1 teaspoon

PROCEDURE

1. Mix Seasoning ingredients together. Roll chicken slices in seasoning until well covered.
2. Add walnuts to batter. Cover chicken slices with batter and deep fry in hot oil until golden brown.
3. To serve, garnish with cucumber and tomato pieces.

Servings: Five to Six

CRISPY CHICKEN
炸子肥雞

Ingredients
1 chicken	3 lbs.
Malt or honey	2 tablespoons
Malt vinegar	2 teaspoons
White vinegar	4 tablespoons
Water	4 tablespoons

Seasoning
Ginger juice	1 teaspoon
Salt	1 tablespoon

Fried Salt
Salt	2 tablespoons
Five Spices powder	1 teaspoon

PROCEDURE
1. Heat 6 cups boiling water and parboil chicken for 20 minutes. Drain and wash well with cold water.
2. Mix vinegars, malt and water, heat over boiling water. Dry chicken with a towel, and rub well with malt mixture. Put salt and ginger juice inside the chicken. Put in a windy place and let dry thoroughly —perhaps overnight.
3. Put a *Chinese spoon inside the chicken, and keep pouring hot oil through the spoon into the chicken's body, allowing it to drain from the neck. Repeat 4 times, then pour hot oil on to the outside of the chicken, until the chicken is golden brown.
4. To serve, chop chicken into pieces and place on platter. Mix fried salt ingredients and warm in hot pan, no oil, and put in separate dish for dip. Shrimp pieces are an interesting garnish.

Servings: Four to Six
*See glossary.

SMOKED SHREDDED CHICKEN
手撕燻雞

Ingredients
1 Chicken	
Broth	1 tin.
Sugar, or granulated sugar	2 pieces.
Tea leaves	4 tablespoons
Pineapple	1 tin.

Seasoning
Root ginger	1 piece
Spice powder	$\frac{1}{4}$ teaspoon

Sauce
Water or broth	$1\frac{1}{2}$ cups
Sauce 1. Dark soy	$\frac{1}{2}$ cup
Sauce 2. Light soy	1 cup
Wine	2 tablespoons
Sugar	$\frac{1}{2}$ cup
Ginger	1 piece
Spring onion	2 stalks
Aniseed	4 pieces

PROCEDURE
1. Clean chicken rub it dry and put a little spice powder and ginger inside.
2. Bring sauce to boil and cook chicken for 25 minutes, drain, and brush with sesame oil.
3. Put foil paper over wok or pan and sprinkle crushed cube sugar and tea leaves.
4. Put chicken on top of a stand or grill, cover tightly and let it smoke for 6 minutes. Shred chicken by hand into pieces and garnish with pineapple and parsley.
5. Serve together with mixture of 3 tablespoons light soy, 1 teaspoon sesame oil and 1 tablespoon chopped onions.

Servings: Four to Six

SHREDDED CHICKEN WITH JELLY SHEETS

海浙雞絲

Ingredients

Chicken fillet	10–12 ozs.
*Jelly sheets	4 ozs.
Cucumber, skinned and shredded	4 ozs.
Sesame seeds, fried until light brown	2 ozs.
Ginger juice	1 tablespoon

Sauce

Light soy sauce	4 tablespoons
Spring onion	3 stalks
Parsley	$\frac{1}{2}$ oz.
Dark vinegar	2 tablespoons
Monosodium glutamate	1 teaspoon
Sesame oil	1 teaspoon
Chilli	1 teaspoon
Sugar	1 teaspoon
*Plum sauce, Hoi Sin sauce	2 tablespoons

PROCEDURE

1. Season chicken breasts with 1 tablespoon salt, 1 tablespoon ginger juice and let stand for 15 minutes. Steam over boiling water for 15 minutes, then cut into shredded pieces.
2. Cut jelly sheets into narrow strips and mix well with a teaspoon salt.
3. Put shredded chicken on top of jelly sheets.
4. Put jelly pieces, cucumber and chicken fillet on a serving dish, pour sauce on top before serving. Garnish with sesame seeds.

Servings: Five to Six
*See glossary.

CHICKEN WING WITH ORANGE SAUCE

香橙雞翼

Ingredients

Chicken wing	16 pieces
Fat pork	4 small slices
Root ginger, sliced	8 pieces
Orange, sliced	1
Sugar, or 2 tablespoons granulated sugar	$1\frac{1}{2}$ pieces

Seasoning

Wine	2 tablespoons
Salt	1 teaspoon
Dark soy sauce	2 tablespoons

Sauce

Broth, or water and chicken cube	$1\frac{1}{2}$ cups
Cornstarch, use afterwards— blend with 2 tablespoons water	$1\frac{1}{2}$ tablespoons
Wine	1 teaspoon

PROCEDURE

1. Put chicken wings in boiling water for 2 minutes. Then drain away water. Dry with a towel.
2. Season with the above seasoning and let soak for 10 minutes.
3. Put fat pork at the bottom of a pot and fry chicken wings for 1 minute. Add ginger pieces, sugar and sliced orange on top.
4. Cook chicken wings together with sauce for 10 minutes (high heat) then simmer for 2–3 minutes, add cornstarch.

How to serve: Chop away the small pointed part of the wings. The cooked, sliced ginger and orange placed on the dish should be covered by the wings. Pour sauce on top.

Servings: Four

BRAISED CHICKEN CUBES WITH BEAN SAUCE

翡翠柱侯雞

Ingredients

Chicken fillet, cut into cubes	1 lb.
*Mustard green, or other green vegetable	1¼ lbs.
Shallots	1 teaspoon
Garlic	1 teaspoon
Root ginger	1 piece
Spring onion	1 stalk
Oil for cooking	
Water	3–4 cups
Pinch of bicarbonate of soda	
salt	½ tablespoon

Seasoning

Light soy sauce	1½ tablespoons
Wine	1 tablespoon
Ginger juice	1 teaspoon
Salt	1 teaspoon
Sesame oil	¼ teaspoon
Water	½ tablespoon
Oil	½ tablespoon

Sauce

Bean paste	1 tablespoon
Water	4 tablespoons
Chicken cube	1
Light soy sauce	1 teaspoon
Sugar	1 tablespoon
Wine	2 tablespoons
Cornstarch, use later	1 teaspoon

PROCEDURE

1. Marinate chicken cubes in the seasoning for 10 minutes.
2. Heat 5 cups boiling oil and quick fry chicken cubes for 1–2 minutes. Drain and empty all the oil, except for 1 tablespoon. Fry bean paste and chicken cubes again for 1 minute. Add sauce. Mix well and it is ready to serve together with the green vegetable.
3. To cook mustard greens (or other green vegetable) add water, 2 tablespoons oil, bicarbonate of soda and salt. Cook greens for 3 minutes. Drain and place chicken on top of the vegetable.

Servings: Four
*Broccoli.

FRIED CHICKEN CUBES WITH PEPPER

彩鳳朝陽

Ingredients

Chicken fillet	1 lb.
Green pepper, cut into triangles	2 ozs.
Red chilli	2 ozs.
Root ginger, shredded	2 pieces
Oil for cooking	

Seasoning

Light soy sauce	2 tablespoons
Cornstarch	1 tablespoon
Sesame oil	½ teaspoon
Pepper	¼ teaspoon
Sugar	½ teaspoon
Salt	½ teaspoon
Water	1 tablespoon
Oil, cooked	1 tablespoon

Sauce

Water or broth	3 tablespoons
Sesame oil	½ tablespoon
Cornstarch	1 teaspoon
Dark soy sauce	½ teaspoon

PROCEDURE

1. Cut chicken fillet into big square cubes and put into seasoning. Marinate, and let stand for 10 minutes.
2. Heat 2 tablespoons oil, stir fry green pepper with a pinch of salt. Remove to a plate.
3. Heat 3 cups oil and quickly-fry chicken cubes until 60% cooked, then drain.
4. Heat 2 tablespoons oil in a pan or wok, brown

Servings: Six to Eight

TUNG KONG CHICKEN

東江鹽水雞

Ingredients

Chicken	2½ lbs.
Root ginger, grated	1 oz.
Root ginger	1 piece
Yellow ginger powder	1 tablespoon
Parsley	½ oz.
Spring onion	2 stalks

Seasoning

Root ginger	1 piece
Salt	1 tablespoon

Sauce

1. Root ginger, chopped fine or grated	1–2 ozs.
Spring onion, chopped finely	2 stalks
Oil, cooked	2 tablespoons
Salt	½ teaspoon
2. Monosodium glutamate	2 teaspoons
Water	3 tablespoons
Oil, cooked	1 tablespoon
Sesame oil	1 teaspoon

PROCEDURE

1. Heat 6 cups of boiling water, add 1 teaspoon monosodium glutamate and 1 tablespoon salt. Rub chicken dry with a towel and put a piece of ginger inside chicken. Cook chicken in the salty water. Lower the heat for 20 minutes, drain.
2. Wash chicken with cold water, so that the skin will be crisp, drain.
3. Cook No. 2 sauce and sprinkle over chicken.
4. Chop chicken into pieces. Use No.1 sauce or yellow ginger powder mixed with 2 tablespoons oil as a dip. Serve garnished with parsley.

Servings: Six

Note: Southern Chinese cooking includes dishes from Canton, Swatow and Tung Kong.

ROAST TURKEY (CHINESE STYLE)

中式燒火雞

Ingredients

1 Turkey	13–15 lbs.
Spring onion	2 stalks
Root ginger, chopped	1 piece

Seasoning for Stuffing

Cooked glutinous rice	1½ lb.
Chopped roast duck, fried	1 lb.
Shallots, chopped finely	1½ tablespoons
Giblets of turkey, chop finely	2–3 ozs.
Mushroom, chopped finely	2 ozs.
Egg, beaten	1
Oil	2 tablespoons
Salt and pepper to taste	
Celery salt	¼ teaspoon
Light soy sauce	2 tablespoons
Monosodium glutamate	1 teaspoon

Sauce

Onions, chopped	3 tablespoons
Flour or cornstarch	1 tablespoon
Salt	1 teaspoon
Pepper	1¼ teaspoons
Dark soy sauce	1 tablespoon
Broth	1 cup

PROCEDURE

1. Wash turkey, and rub dry. Put inside pepper, ginger and spring onions. Stand for ½ hour.
2. Mix stuffing ingredients together and fill neck cavity with stuffing, but do not stuff too full. Sew up cavity.
3. Heat oven for 20 minutes before roasting. The quick way to get a turkey roasted well is to cook and brown the breast in 450°F heat for 30 mins, then turn over and brown the back for 20 minutes. Cover with a piece of foil paper and roast for another hour.
4. Cook the juice from the turkey together with the sauce ingredients, until the mixture thickens.
5. Garnish with red chilli and parsley and serve with onion sauce.

Servings: Twelve

WHOLE CHICKEN BAKED IN SALT
正式鹽焗雞

Ingredients
Chicken	2½ lbs.
*Sand salt, coarse	5 lbs.
Root ginger	2 pieces.
Spring Onion	1 stalk
Wine	1 tablespoon
Salt	1 teaspoon
Light soy sauce	1 tablespoon
Sugar	1 teaspoon
Aniseed and dried chilli	1 teaspoon

PROCEDURE
1. Rub and dry chicken.
2. Season inside of chicken with wine, salt, sugar, aniseed and dried chilli, then rub skin with light soy sauce.
3. Fry salt for 10 minutes.
4. Soak 2 big pieces of thin Chinese mulberry paper in oil. Squeeze dry and wrap chicken with it. Put wrapped chicken in a pan and cover with hot fried salt at bottom and on top. Put the pan into the stove for 1 hour.
5. To serve, cut chicken into pieces.

Servings: Four to Six
*Rock salt.

MINCED CHICKEN WITH SPINACH
雞茸波菜

Ingredients
Chicken fillet, minced	½ lb.
Spinach	8 ozs.
Garlic, chopped	1 teaspoon
Oil for cooking	

Seasoning
Salt	1 teaspoon
Sesame oil	½ teaspoon
Cornstarch	½ tablespoon
Water	½ tablespoon
Oil	½ tablespoon

Sauce
Water or broth	1 cup
Cornstarch	1 tablespoon
Sesame oil	½ teaspoon
Salt	1 teaspoon

PROCEDURE
1. Heat 2 tablespoons oil, brown ½ teaspoon garlic and fry spinach for 2–3 minutes. Add 4 tablespoons water and 1 teaspoon salt. Cook again for 2–3 minutes. Drain and remove to a plate.
2. Heat 2 tablespoons oil, add garlic, then minced chicken. Stir fry for 2–3 minutes.
3. Add sauce, bring to boil, mix well with one egg white, and pour over vegetable and serve. Chopped ham can be added.

Servings: Two

CABBAGE IN CHICKEN SAUCE (SHANGHAI)
雞油白菜

Ingredients
*Chinese cabbage	1 lb.
*Chinese dried mushroom, soak and remove stem	4 pieces
*Chinese ham, cooked	1 oz.
Dried shrimps, soaked and dried	1 tablespoon
Oil for cooking	
Root ginger	1 piece

Sauce
Broth	½ cup
Salt	1 teaspoon
Monosodium glutamate	½ teaspoon
Cornstarch	½ tablespoon
(Melted chicken fat optional)	
Wine	1 tablespoon

PROCEDURE
1. Wash cabbage and cut into 2″ sections. Cook cabbage with 5 cups boiling water for 3 minutes then remove from stove.
2. Heat 2 tablespoons oil in pan, stir fry ginger, mushrooms, ham and dried shrimps for 1 minute.
3. Toss and mix well with cabbage. Add wine and sauce and it is ready to serve.

Servings: Four to Five
*See glossary.

CHICKEN CUBES WITH ASPARAGUS

露筍雞球

Ingredients

Chicken fillet, cut into cubes	12 ozs.
Asparagus, fresh	8 ozs.
Spring onion, cut into sections	2 stalks
Root ginger	1 piece
Carrots	4 pieces

Seasoning

(For chicken)

Light soy sauce	2 tablespoons
Cornstarch	1 tablespoon
Sesame oil	$\frac{1}{2}$ teaspoon
Pepper	$\frac{1}{2}$ teaspoon
Sugar	$\frac{1}{2}$ teaspoon
Salt	1 teaspoon
Oil	1 tablespoon
Water	1 tablespoon

Sauce

Chicken broth	3 tablespoons
Sesame oil	$\frac{1}{4}$ teaspoon
Light soy sauce	1 teaspoon
Cornstarch	1 teaspoon
Monosodium glutamate	1 teaspoon

PROCEDURE

1. Heat boiling water, add 2 tablespoons oil and 1 tablespoon salt, and cook fresh asparagus for 3 minutes. Drain and remove to a plate.

2. Mix seasoning ingredients together. Roll chicken pieces in seasoning until well covered.

3. Heat 3 tablespoons oil, brown spring onions and shallots, Stir fry chicken cubes for 2 minutes. Add sauce and put on top of asparagus, ready to serve.

Servings: Four

Note: 1. Two tablespoons of oyster sauce can be added to sauce to enrich flavour.

2. One tablespoon of Shanghai Chilli can be added to the sauce to get hot effect.

BEGGAR'S CHICKEN

富貴大雞

Ingredients

One chicken	3 lbs.
Dried lotus leaves, soaked in in boiling water	2 pieces
*Preserved Chinese vegetable shredded	3 ozs.
Lean pork, shredded	2 ozs.
Fat pork, shredded	3 ozs.
Root ginger, shredded	1 piece
Spring onion	2 stalks
*Mud, from yellow wine jar	2 lbs.

Seasoning

Wine	2 tablespoons
Light soy sauce	1 tablespoon
Sugar	1 tablespoon
Sesame oil	$\frac{1}{2}$ teaspoon

PROCEDURE

1. Clean chicken, rub it dry and season the skin with 1 tablespoon dark soy sauce.

2. Heat 2 tablespoons oil, fry the seasoned stuffing ingredients for 2–3 minutes.

3. Put all the stuffing ingredients inside the chicken and wrap well in a parcel with lotus leaves, then wrap again with newspaper or with wet mulberry paper.

4. Pound mud, and mix with a little water until wet, cover the parcel with mud and wrap in thin absorbent paper.

5. Heat the oven until hot (350°F) and bake chicken for $2\frac{1}{2}$ hours.

6. Break the mud from the beggar's chicken with a wooden hammer and unwrap chicken from lotus leaves, ready to serve.

Servings: Four to Six
*See glossary.

WEST LAKE DUCK
西湖鴨

Ingredient
1 Duck	$2\frac{1}{2}$ lbs.
Parsley, shredded	2–3 ozs.
Bamboo shoots, shredded	2 ozs.
Lean Pork, shredded	4 ozs.
Mushroom, shredded, season with wine and sugar	4 pieces

Seasoning
Dark soy sauce	2 tablespoons
Root ginger	1 piece
Spring onion	1 stalk
Salt	1 teaspoon

Sauce
Water	$\frac{3}{4}$ cup
Dark soy sauce	1 teaspoon
Sesame oil	1 teaspoon
Sugar	$\frac{1}{2}$ teaspoon
Chicken cube, or 1 teaspoon monosodium glutamate	
Cornstarch	$\frac{1}{2}$ tablespoon

PROCEDURE
1. Clean duck and rub dry. Mix seasoning ingredients to-gether. Roll duck in seasoning until covered, then deep fry until golden brown.
2. Steam duck over boiling water for $1\frac{1}{2}$ hours.
3. Heat 2 tablespoons oil and stir fry the parsley, bamboo shoots, lean pork and mushrooms. Add sauce and bring to boil and pour over duck.

Servings: Five to Six

STEWED DUCK WITH TARO
芋頭炆鴨

Ingredients
1 whole or $\frac{1}{2}$ duck	$2\frac{1}{2}$ lb.
*Taro, cooked and cut up	1 lb.
Root ginger	1 oz.
Spring onion	2 stalks

Seasoning
Dark soy sauce	2 tablespoons
Wine	1 tablespoon
Pepper	$\frac{1}{4}$ teaspoon

Sauce
Bean paste	3 tablespoons
Sesame paste	1 tablespoon
Sugar	3 tablespoons
Wine	2 tablespoons
Water	3 cups
Chicken cube	1

PROCEDURE
1. Clean duck and rub dry. Cover with seasoning.
2. Deep fry until skin is golden brown.
3. Drain and steam duck together with taro over boiling water for $1\frac{1}{2}$ hours.
4. Heat 3 tablespoons oil, fry ginger, spring onions, bean paste and sesame paste. Add duck cut in halves with taro and cook together with the above sauce for 15 minutes, then thicker with cornstarch.

Servings: Six to Seven
*Sweet Potato—cook for $\frac{1}{2}$ hour.

FRIED DUCK WITH ONION SAUCE
洋葱大鴨

Ingredients
Duck, one or half	3 lbs.
Onion, small	$\frac{3}{4}$–1 lb.

Seasoning
Dark soy sauce	2 tablespoons
Wine	1 tablespoon
Ginger juice	1 tablespoon
Pepper	$\frac{1}{4}$ teaspoon
Salt	1 teaspoon
Root ginger	1 piece

Sauce
Water	1$\frac{1}{2}$ cups
Chicken cube, chopped	1
Oil	$\frac{1}{2}$ teaspoon
Cornstarch, use later	1 tablespoon
Sugar	1 teaspoon
Salt	1 teaspoon

PROCEDURE
1. Clean duck, rub it dry with a towel, and marinate with the above seasoning for 15 minutes.
2. Heat 4–5 cups oil and quick fry onions, drain.
3. Deep fry duck in hot oil, then remove to a pot, steam over boiling water until tender. Lower the heat, add onions and steam for another 15 minutes.
4. Chop duck into pieces and remove to a plate. Bring sauce to boil and pour on top of duck.

To serve: Garnish with parsley. Arranged cooked onions on both sides of the duck on the plate.

Servings: Six to Eight

LO HON DUCK
羅漢扒鴨

Ingredients
1 Duck	3 lbs.
Seasonal vegetable	2 ozs.
Mushroom, soaked, remove stem	10 pieces
Champignon, sliced	1 tin
Peanuts, remove shell	2 oz.
Olive seed, fried	1 oz.
Fungus, soaked in water	$\frac{1}{4}$ oz.
Bamboo shoots, sliced	2 ozs.
Green peas	3 ozs.
Bean sprout	2 ozs.

Seasoning
Dark soy sauce	1 tablespoon
Ginger juice	1 tablespoon
Wine	1 tablespoon
Salt	$\frac{1}{2}$ teaspoon

Sauce
Water, or chicken broth	1$\frac{1}{2}$ cups
Chicken cube	1
Sesame oil	$\frac{1}{4}$ teaspoon
Oyster sauce	2 tablespoons
Sugar	1 teaspoon
Cornstarch, use later	1 tablespoon

PROCEDURE
1. Season duck with seasoning.
2. Steam duck over boiling water for 1$\frac{1}{2}$ hours.
3. Heat 2 tablespoons oil and fry all other ingredients. Add sauce, bring to boil for 5 minutes then add cornstarch. Pour on top of duck and serve. Arrange green vegetable on both sides of duck.

Servings: Six to Eight

Beef and Pork
豬，牛．

Pork is the main meat used in traditional Chinese cooking

and can be prepared in many different ways.

Sauces and vegetables are used to vary the flavour to

suit the type of dish being prepared.

Beef is not a traditional ingredient of Chinese cooking

but is being used increasingly particularly in

dishes prepared for the Western palate.

Meat is usually cut into small pieces

which allows for quick cooking and the easy blending

of other ingredients.

The important thing to remember in cooking meats

as with vegetables is *never to overcook*.

SHREDDED BEEF AND PEPPER (Capsicum)

青椒牛肉絲

Ingredients

Loin beef, shredded	12 ozs.
Carrots, shredded	1 cup
Pepper, seeded and shredded	1 cup
Garlic, chopped finely	1 teaspoon
Oil for cooking	

Seasoning

Light soy sauce	2 tablespoons
Cornstarch	1 tablespoon
Oil	1 tablespoon
Water	1 tablespoon
Pepper	$\frac{1}{5}$ teaspoon

Sauce

Chicken broth, or water and monosodium glutamate	2 tablespoons
Sesame oil	2 drops
Dark soy sauce	$\frac{1}{2}$ teaspoon
Salt	pinch

PROCEDURE

1. Heat 2 tablespoons oil and when very hot. Stir fry shredded carrots and pepper. Add 1 teaspoon salt and sprinkle $\frac{1}{2}$ tablespoon water. Remove to a plate.
2. Heat 3–4 tablespoons oil. When oil is hot, add garlic, then stir. Fry shredded beef for 2–3 minutes. Add sauce and mix well with the carrots and peppers.

Servings: Four

BEEF FILLET WITH PEAS

青豆牛肉

Ingredients

Green peas	4 ozs
Beef steak	12 ozs.
Root ginger, shredded	1 piece
Scallion, chopped	1 stalk
Oil for cooking	

Seasoning

Dark soy sauce	2 tablespoons
Cornstarch	1 tablespoon
Pepper	$\frac{1}{4}$ teaspoon
Sesame oil	$\frac{1}{4}$ teaspoon
Sugar	pinch
Water	1 tablespoon
Oil	1 tablespoon

Sauce

Chicken broth	3 tablespoons
Cornstarch	$\frac{1}{2}$ teaspoon
Sesame oil	3–4 drops
Oyster sauce, optional	1 tablespoon

PROCEDURE

1. Cut beef fillet into $2'' \times 1'' \times \frac{1}{2}''$ pieces and marinate in seasoning. Stand for 15 minutes.
2. Heat oil in a large frying pan and when hot, add ginger (or garlic) and fry beef for $\frac{1}{2}$ minute.
3. Add sauce and peas, mix well over high heat, remove to a plate and serve. Garnish with parsley.

Servings: Four

FRIED BEEF WITH VEGETABLE

時菜牛肉

Ingredients

Beef fillet, sliced	12 ozs.
Seasonal vegetables	1 lb.
Root ginger	2 pieces
Garlic	2 cloves
Water	1 tablespoon
Bicarbonate of soda	1 teaspoon

Seasoning

Dark soy sauce	1 tablespoon
Sugar	1 teaspoon
Salt	$\frac{1}{2}$ teaspoon
Water	1 tablespoon
Peanut oil	1 tablespoon
Pepper	$\frac{1}{4}$ teaspoon
Wine	1 teaspoon
Sesame oil	$\frac{1}{2}$ teaspoon
Cornstarch	1 tablespoon

Sauce

Chicken broth	$\frac{1}{2}$ cup
Cornstarch	1 teaspoon
Light soy sauce	1 teaspoon
Sugar	$\frac{1}{2}$ teaspoon
Salt, to taste	
Sesame oil, a few drops	

PROCEDURE

1. Cut beef fillet into 1 inch slices.
2. Season with the above seasoning and allow to soak for $\frac{1}{2}$ hour.
3. Heat oil, brown garlic and cook vegetables for 5 minutes with $\frac{1}{2}$ cup broth. Drain and remove to a plate.
4. Heat oil, brown garlic, add shredded ginger, and fry beef for 3 minutes. Put in sauce and it is ready to serve over vegetables.

Servings: Four

STEWED BEEF IN POT

傑仔牛腩

Ingredients

Beef, shin	1½ lbs.
Root ginger	3 pieces
Aniseed	4 pieces
Spring onions,	2 stalks
cut into sections	4 ozs.
Soy bean paste	1 tablespoon
Bean paste	2 tablespoons
Onions chopped	4 tablespoons

Sauce

Water	4–5 cups
Chicken cube	1 cube
Light soy sauce	2 tablespoons
Dark soy sauce	3 tablespoons
Wine	1 tablespoon
Sugar	1 tablespoon
Cornstarch	1½ tablespoons

PROCEDURE

1. Put pieces of beef into boiling water together with 1 piece ginger and two stalks spring onions, 1 tablespoon wine. Cook for 5 minutes. Drain and cut beef into 2-inch pieces.
2. Heat 2 tablespoons oil, brown ginger, onions and soy bean paste and stir fry beef pieces. Pour in sauce, and aniseed. Stew for 1½ hours.
3. Add cornstarch and sprinkle a few drops of sesame oil before serving.

Variation: Bamboo shoots or carrots can be added 10 minutes before serving.

Servings: Six

BEEF FILLET WITH EGGS

滑蛋牛肉

Ingredients

Beef fillet	10 ozs.
Eggs	6
Root ginger	2 pieces
Spring onion, or onion	2 stalks
Garlic	1 piece
Bicarbonate of soda	½ teaspoon
Water	1 tablespoon

Seasoning

Dark soy sauce	2 tablespoons
Sesame oil	¼ teaspoon
Pepper	¼ teaspoon
Water	2 tablespoons
Oil	2 tablespoons
Sugar	1 teaspoon
Sesame oil	1 teaspoon

PROCEDURE

1. Cut beef fillet into 1½-inch slices and season with the above seasoning and allow to absorb for 1 hour. Put into the refrigerator.
2. Beat eggs together with 1 teaspoon salt.
3. Heat 4–5 tablespoons oil, brown ginger and spring onions and stir fry beef fillet. Pour in beaten eggs and mix well together. To serve, garnish with parsley.

Servings: Six

BRAISED TONGUE WITH TOMATO SAUCE

西汁燴牛脷

Ingredients

Ox tongue	1½ lb.
Root ginger	2 pieces
Spring onion	2 stalks
Onion, cut into cubes	4 ozs.
Tomato, cut into sections	4 ozs.
Wine	2 tablespoons
Green pepper, chopped	2 ozs.

Seasoning

Salt	1 tablespoon
Wine	2 tablespoons

Sauce

Water	1½ cups
Tomato	4 ozs.
Tomato sauce	3 tablespoons
Tomato puree	1 tablespoon
Salt	½ teaspoon
Sugar	1 tablespoon
Light soy sauce	1 tablespoon
Sesame oil	¼ teaspoon
Pepper	¼ teaspoon
Wine	1 teaspoon
Cornstarch	1 tablespoon

PROCEDURE

1. Heat boiling water in a pot and cook ox tongue for 10 minutes drain. Scrape, clean and rub dry.
2. Marinate ox tongue in seasoning for 10 minutes and cook in boiling water (10 cups) with ginger and spring onions for about 1½ hours. Slice into pieces.
3. Heat 3 tablespoons oil in wok, brown spring onion and tomatoes. Add sauce, bring to boil and cook together with ox tongue and peppers.
4. Before serving, add ½ teaspoon oil.

Servings: Six to Eight

BEEF FILLET WITH BROCCOLI
芥蘭牛肉

Ingredients

Broccoli, sections	8 ozs.
Beef fillet, sliced, 1½″ pieces	8–10 ozs.
Spring onion, cut into sections	4 stalks
Root ginger, shredded	1 piece

Seasoning

Water	1 tablespoon
Bicarbonate of soda	½ teaspoon
Dark soy sauce	2 tablespoons
Cornstarch	1 tablespoon
Sesame oil	1 teaspoon
Sugar	1 teaspoon
Water	1 tablespoon
Pepper	¼ teaspoon
Oil	1 teaspoon

Sauce

Water	4 tablespoons
Sesame oil	½ teaspoon
Oyster sauce	1 tablespoon
Cornstarch	1 teaspoon

PROCEDURE

1. Heat boiling water and cook vegetables for 3 minutes together with one tablespoon wine, 1 tablespoon salt, 2 tablespoons oil and a pinch of cooking soda. Put on a plate.
2. Season sliced beef with the above, and quick deep fry in oil for 1 minute. Drain.
3. Heat 2 tablespoons oil and stir fry garlic, adding beef. Add sauce, mix well and pour over vegetables to serve.

Servings: Four

SHREDDED BEEF FILLET WITH BABY CORN
粟米牛柳絲

Ingredients

Beef fillet, shredded	8–10 ozs.
Baby corn, drained	1 tin
Celery, shredded	½ oz.
Carrot, cut into slices	2 ozs.
Garlic, chopped	½ teaspoon

Seasoning

Bicarbonate of soda	½ teaspoon
Water	1 tablespoon
Cornstarch	1 tablespoon
Oil	1 tablespoon
Pepper	1 teaspoon
Sesame oil	1 teaspoon
Sugar	½ teaspoon
Dark soy sauce	2 tablespoons

Sauce

Water	3 tablespoons
monosodium glutamate	½ teaspoon
Sesame oil	¼ teaspoon
Sugar	¼ teaspoon

PROCEDURE

1. Heat 2 tablespoons oil and brown garlic. Stir fry baby corn, add ½ teaspoon monosodium glutamate and water. Cook for 1 minute and remove to a plate.
2. Season beef fillet with the above seasoning and and quick deep fry in 4 cups of oil for 1 minute. Drain.
3. Heat 1 tablespoon oil, stir fry beef again and mix well with baby corn, celery and carrot. Add sauce.

Servings: Four

Variation: For soft and tender beef, after marinading with the above seasoning, freeze it for 1 hour (or even overnight). The cooked meat will melt in your month.

Fried Beef with Vegetables ▶

Overpage Left: Rainbow Meat
Overpage Right: Sweet and Sour Pork

FRIED BEEF WITH PINEAPPLE

菠蘿牛肉

Ingredients

Pineapple, cored and sliced	1
Beef fillet, sliced	12–16 ozs.
Red and green pepper, chopped	3 ozs.
Young root ginger, chopped	2 ozs.
Oil for cooking	

Seasoning

Water	1 tablespoon
Cooking soda	1 teaspoon
Cornstarch	$1\frac{1}{2}$ tablespoons
Dark soy sauce	2 tablespoons
Sesame oil	$\frac{1}{2}$ teaspoon

GOLD AND SILVER BEEF

金銀牛肉

Ingredients

Beef fillet	8 ozs.
Bean sprout	4 ozs.
Chives or spring onion	1 oz.
*Fried Chinese dumplings	2 ozs.
Garlic, chopped	1 teaspoon
Root ginger	2 pieces

Seasoning

Bicarbonate of soda	$\frac{1}{2}$ teaspoon
Water	1 tablespoon
Dark soy sauce	2 tablespoons
Cornstarch	1 tablespoon
Egg white	1 egg
Water	1 tablespoon
Oil	1 tablespoon
Pepper	$\frac{1}{2}$ teaspoon
Sugar	1 teaspoon

SLICED BEEF WITH POTATO SLICES

薯仔牛柳

Ingredients

Beef fillet	8–10 ozs.
Potatoes	6 ozs.
Oil for cooking	

Seasoning

Dark soy sauce	1 tablespoon
Cornstarch	1 tablespoon
Sesame oil	$\frac{1}{2}$ teaspoon
Pepper	$\frac{1}{5}$ teaspoon
Water	1 tablespoon
Oil	1 tablespoon
Spring onions	4 ozs.
Wine	1 teaspoon

Pepper	$\frac{1}{4}$ teaspoon
Sugar	$\frac{1}{2}$ teaspoon

Sauce

Water	1 tablespoon
Monosodium glutamate	$\frac{1}{5}$ teaspoon
Sesame oil	2 drops
Light soy sauce	1 teaspoon

PROCEDURE

1. Season beef slices with water and cooking soda for 1 hour. Then add the rest of the seasoning.
2. Heat 1 tablespoon boiling oil. Fry peppers and shallots, then mix well with beef slices and stir fry for 1 minute. Add pineapple. Mix well and serve.
3. Use the hollow pineapple as serving dish.

Sauce

Broth or water	$\frac{1}{2}$ cup
Cornstarch	1 teaspoon
Light soy sauce	1 teaspoon
Wine	1 teaspoon

PROCEDURE

1. Cut beef fillet into shredded thin pieces. Season with the above seasoning for 1 hour.
2. Cut Chinese fried dumplings into $\frac{2}{5}$ inch thick pieces and deep fry for 1 minute. Drain oil and remove to a plate.
3. Heat pan, add 1 tablespoon oil, then pour away the oil. Fry bean sprouts with a little salt and wine for 1 minute. Remove to a plate.
4. Heat 4 cups oil, quick fry beef slices for 2 minutes, drain.
5. Heat 2 tablespoons oil and put in garlic. Fry beef for 5 minutes and mix with chives, root ginger and sauce. To serve, pour over fried dumplings.

*Fried potatoes can be substituted.
Servings: Four to Six

Sauce

Water	4 tablespoons
Cornstarch	$\frac{3}{4}$ teaspoon
Sesame oil	$\frac{1}{5}$ teaspoon
Monosodium glutamate	pinch.

PROCEDURE

1. Slice beef thinly and marinate in seasoning. Stand for $\frac{1}{2}$ hour.
2. Peel and slice potatoes. Rinse in cold water and dry with towel.
3. Heat 5 cups oil and deep fry potatoes until golden brown. Drain and remove to a plate.
4. Heat 4 tablespoons oil, add spring onions and saute beef for 2 minutes. Add sauce, mix well and pour over fried potatoes. Garnish with parsley.

Servings: Four

◀ Stewed Lion's Head

HOT AND SOUR SPARE RIBS

酸辣排骨

Ingredients

Spare ribs	3 lbs.

Seasoning

Salt	1 teaspoon
Garlic, chopped	2 cloves
Root ginger, chopped	2 slices
Onions, chopped finely	4 tablespoons
Sugar	3 teaspoons
Soy sauce	4 tablespoons
Sherry	3 tablespoons
*Hoi Sin Sauce	3 tablespoons
Chilli sauce	2 tablespoons
Dark vinegar	2 tablespoons
Pepper	$\frac{1}{2}$ teaspoon
Oil	4 tablespoons
Broth	1 cup

PROCEDURE

1. Cut the spare ribs into individual ribs and rub with salt.
2. Heat oil in a frying pan or wok, add ginger, onion and garlic and fry together. Then add the ribs and stir fry for 5 minutes.
3. Add the rest of the sauce and keep on frying. Then add broth and lower heat and simmer. Cover and cook for 20 minutes. Uncover, mix well and cook for another 10 minutes.
4. Spread all the ribs onto a roasting pan and put in an oven to roast over medium heat for 10 minutes.

Servings: Six to Seven
*See glossary.

FRIED SPICY PORK CHOP

五香豬排

Ingredients

Pork chops, sliced and beaten with tenderiser	1 lb.
Tomato	6 pieces

Seasoning

Light soy sauce	3 tablespoons
Cornstarch	2 tablespoons
Pepper	$\frac{1}{4}$ teaspoon
Five-spice powder	$\frac{1}{2}$ teaspoon
Salt	1 teaspoon
Sugar	$\frac{1}{2}$ teaspoon
Water	1 tablespoon
Oil	1 tablespoon
Egg, beaten	1

To make spicy salt

Heat salt	1 tablespoon
and five-spice powder	$\frac{1}{2}$ teaspoon

PROCEDURE

1. Marinate sliced pork chops with the above seasoning for $\frac{1}{2}$ hour.
2. Heat a lot of oil and deep fry until golden brown.
3. Garnish with tomato slices and dip with fried spicy salt.

Servings: Six

RAINBOW MEAT

七彩鬆

Ingredients

Lean Pork, chopped finely	8 ozs.
Bamboo shoot, chopped finely	4 ozs.
Celery, chopped finely	2 ozs.
Carrots, chopped finely	2 ozs.
Dried mushroom, chopped finely	8 pieces
Garlic	1 teaspoon
*Olive seed, fried and crushed	2 ozs.
Lettuce cups, for wrapping	1 lb.
Hoi Sin sauce	4 tablespoons

Seasoning

Salt	$\frac{1}{2}$ teaspoon
Sugar	$\frac{1}{2}$ teaspoon
Light soy sauce	2 tablespoons
Cornstarch	1 tablespoon
Wine	1 teaspoon
Sesame oil	$\frac{1}{2}$ teaspoon

PROCEDURE

1. Put bamboo shoots, celery, dried mushrooms and carrots in a wok or pan and dry up the water with low heat.
2. Heat oil (2 tablespoons) and stir fry the above. Add 1 teaspoon salt, then remove to a plate.
3. Heat 2 tablespoons oil, brown onions together with lean pork and stir fry for 2–3 minutes, until the meat changes to a white colour. Add fried, crushed olive seeds on top.

To serve: Take lettuce cup and put one tablespoon of 'rainbow' meat in and wrap well. Serve with $\frac{1}{2}$ teaspoon Hoi Sin sauce.

Servings: Four to Six
*See glossary.

QUICK FRIED BEEF SLICES WITH ONIONS

洋葱牛肉

Ingredients

Beef fillet	12 ozs.
Onions, shredded	4 ozs.
Root ginger, shredded	1 piece
Spring onions, chopped	1 stalk

Seasoning
(for beef)

Water	1 tablespoon
Bicarbonate of soda	$\frac{1}{2}$ teaspoon
Dark soy sauce	2 tablespoons
Cornstarch	1 tablespoon
Sesame oil	$\frac{1}{4}$ teaspoon
Water	1 tablespoon
Oil	1 tablespoon
Pepper	$\frac{1}{4}$ teaspoon

Sauce

Chicken broth, or water and monosodium glutamate	4 tablespoons
Cornstarch	$\frac{1}{2}$ teaspoon
Dark soy sauce	$\frac{1}{3}$ teaspoon
Sesame oil	2 drops

PROCEDURE

1. Slice beef fillet into thin pieces and marinate in seasoning. Let stand for $\frac{1}{2}$ hour.
2. Heat 4 tablespoons oil, fry beef slices for 2–3 minutes. Add shredded onions, and stir fry again for 2–3 minutes.
3. Add sauce, mix well and serve.

Servings: Four

SLICED COLD BEEF

鹵水牛肉

Ingredients

Beef, shin	2 lbs.
Ginger	2 pieces
Spring onions	2 stalks

Sauce

Chicken broth, or water and chicken cube	5 cups
Dark soy sauce	$\frac{1}{2}$ cup
Sugar	$\frac{1}{2}$ cup
Spring onions	2 stalks
Ginger	2 pieces
Aniseed	3 pieces
Wine	2 tablespoons

PROCEDURE

1. Put shin of beef in boiling water for 5 minutes. Drain.
2. Combine the sauce mixture and bring to boil. Simmer shin of beef in sauce for 1 hour.
3. When cold, put in refrigerator over-night.
4. To served slice into razor-thin pieces.

Servings: Five to Six

BEEF FILLET WITH SCRAMBLED EGGS

滑蛋牛肉

Ingredients

Beef fillet	6 ozs.
Eggs, beaten	4
Onion, shredded	2 ozs.

Seasoning

Water	1 tablespoon
Dark soy sauce	1 tablespoon
Cornstarch	$\frac{1}{2}$ tablespoon
Pepper	$\frac{1}{5}$ teaspoon
Sesame oil	$\frac{1}{5}$ teaspoon
Oil	$\frac{1}{2}$ tablespoon

PROCEDURE

1. Slice beef fillet into $2'' \times 1'' \times \frac{1}{5}''$ slices and marinate in seasoning. Let stand for $\frac{1}{2}$ hour.
2. Heat 3–4 tablespoons oil until it is hot then fry shredded onions and beef slices for 2–3 minutes.
3. Mix with beaten eggs and stir fry for another 1 minute and serve.

Servings: Two

WANTON SOUP WITH VEGETABLE

時菜雲吞湯

Ingredients

(For wanton)

Lean and fat pork, cut into small cubes	6 ozs.
Shrimp, shelled and cut into small pieces	6 ozs.
Egg	1 egg
*Wanton sheets	30 pieces
Vegetables, choysum	4 ozs.
Chives	2 ozs.
Chicken broth and water	1 tin
Oil bicarbonate of soda	

PROCEDURE

(To make wanton)

1. Season pork cubes and shrimps with $\frac{1}{2}$ teaspoon light soy sauce, $\frac{1}{2}$ teaspoon salt, $\frac{1}{4}$ teaspoon sesame oil and $\frac{1}{2}$ egg yolk.

2. Wrap wanton with the above stuffing.

3. Cook wanton in boiling water for 2 minutes, drain and put aside.

4. Cook vegetables in boiling water for 1 minute together with 1 tablespoon oil and a pinch of bicarbonate of soda. Drain.

5. *Procedure to make wanton soup*

Open one tin of chicken broth, add 5 cups boiling water and bring to boil.

6. Add wanton, chives and vegetables to broth and season with 1 tablespoon salt, $\frac{1}{2}$ teaspoon sesame oil, and 1 chicken cube. Bring to boil and serve.

Servings: Four to Six
*Buy from Chinese delicatessen.

ASSORTED MEAT WITH LONG BEAN

清炒五寶鬆

Ingredients

Long bean or string beans, chopped	6 ozs.
Lean pork, cut into cubes	8 ozs.
Mushroom, cut into cubes	6 pieces
Dry shrimp, chopped fine	3 ozs.
*Preserved vegetable, cut into small particles	2 ozs.
*Olive seed, fried and crushed	3 ozs.
Garlic crushed	1 piece

Seasoning

(For lean pork)

Light soy sauce	1 tablespoon
Cornstarch	1 teaspoon
Sesame oil	$\frac{1}{4}$ teaspoon
Pepper	$\frac{1}{4}$ teaspoon
Sugar	$\frac{1}{2}$ teaspoon
Salt	$\frac{1}{4}$ teaspoon
Water	1 tablespoon
Oil	1 tablespoon
(For mushrooms)	
Wine	$\frac{1}{2}$ teaspoon
Sugar	$\frac{1}{4}$ teaspoon

PROCEDURE

1. Fry beans with 2 tablespoon oil and a few drops of water and remove to a plate.

2. Heat 3 tablespoon oil, brown garlic, stir fry lean pork, mushrooms, dried shrimps and preserved vegetables for 2 minutes, then add chilli. Place on top of long beans, sprinkle crushed olive seeds on top. A very tasty dish for the summer.

Servings: Four
*See glossary.

WHITE CUT PORK

蒜子白肉

Ingredients

Leg of pork	2 lbs.
Wine	2 tablespoons
Root ginger	1 piece

Dip

Shrimp sauce	2–3 tablespoons
Oil	1 tablespoon
Soy sauce	3 tablespoons
Garlic, chopped fine	1 tablespoon
Sesame oil	1 teaspoon

PROCEDURE

1. Place the pork in a pan of boiling water and boil for 5 minutes then pour away the water.

2. In a deep pan, add the piece of pork and enough water to cover and bring to the boil. Simmer for 1 hour then add wine and ginger.

3. Remove pan with its contents and allow to cool. When cold, cut the pork into slices, about $2'' \times 1'' \times \frac{1}{4}''$.

To serve: Arrange slices neatly in fish-scale fashion on a plate. Serve dip in individual bowls round pork dish.

SPECIAL PORK CHOPS AND PRAWN BALLS

京都雙拼

SPECIAL PORK CHOPS:

Ingredients

Pork chops cut in 2″ pieces	16 ozs.
Light soy sauce	1 tablespoon
Dark soy sauce	1 tablespoon
Wine	1 tablespoon
Cornstarch	½ tablespoon
Pepper	1 teaspoon
Sugar	1 teaspoon
Garlic	1 tablespoon
Pineapple	4 slices
Oil for cooking	

Sauce

*O.K. Sauce	2 tablespoons
Sugar	2 tablespoons
Wine	1 teaspoon

PROCEDURE

1. Season pork with soy sauce, wine, cornstarch and pepper and allow to stand for about ½ hour.
2. Deep fry pork in 5 cups oil twice until it is golden brown. Drain and remove to a plate.
3. Clean pan and heat 1 tablespoon oil and brown garlic. Add pork chops and mix together with sugar, wine and O.K. sauce.

PRAWN BALLS:

Ingredients:

Shrimp, shelled and mashed	16 ozs.
Spring onion, chopped finely	2 stalks
Egg, beaten	1

Seasoning:

Salt	1 teaspoon
Cornstarch	1 tablespoon
Sesame oil	¼ teaspoon
Pepper	¼ teaspoon

PROCEDURE:

1. Marinate prawns with seasoning and mix well, until crunchy.
2. Roll mixture into balls and dip into beaten egg and rub with a little cornstarch.
3. Heat 4 cups boiling oil and deep fry prawn balls until golden brown and drain.
4. To serve, put Prawn balls on one side of the dish with the special pork chops on the other. Garnish with parsley and pineapple.

Servings: Eight to Ten
*See glossary.

PORK SPARE RIBS WITH CARROT AND TURNIP

金銀蘿蔔排骨湯

Ingredients

Pork spare ribs	1 lb.
Carrots	4 ozs.
Turnips	4 ozs.
Onions	2 ozs.
Chicken broth	2 cups
Water	4 cups
Salt	½ tablespoon
Pepper to taste	
Sesame oil	2–3 drops

PROCEDURE

1. Cut spare ribs into 2″ pieces and trim away any fat.
2. Put 2½ cups boiling water into pot and parboil for 3–4 minutes, then drain.
3. Cut carrots, turnips and onions into triangular wedge-shaped pieces. Add these to the broth, together with the spare ribs and bring to the boil.
4. Let simmer for 35 minutes, season to taste with salt, pepper and sesame oil and serve.

Servings: Four

PORK CHOPS WITH LEMON SAUCE

檸汁豬排

Ingredients

Pork chops, sliced 2″ thick	12 ozs.
Lemon, sliced for garnishing	1 piece
Lemon, juice to make sauce	1 piece
Oil for cooking	

Seasoning

Light soy sauce	2 tablespoons
Cornstarch	1 tablespoon
Egg, beaten	1 piece
Sesame oil	¼ teaspoon
Sugar	½ teaspoon

Sauce

Lemon juice, made from lemon	1 lemon
Sugar	2–3 tablespoons
Water	¾ cup
Cornstarch	1 tablespoon
Dark soy sauce	½ teaspoon

PROCEDURE

1. Marinate pork chops in seasoning. Stand for 10 minutes.
2. Rub pork chop with cornstarch and deep fry in oil until golden brown.
3. Heat 1 tablespoon oil and cook sauce for a minute. Pour over pork chops and serve.
Arrange sliced lemons to garnish.

Servings: Four to Five

SWEET AND SOUR PORK
甜酸咕嚕肉

Ingredients

Lean pork, cut into 1 inch cubes	12 ozs.
Egg	1
Red or green pepper, cut into 1 inch pieces	2
Fresh ginger, chopped finely	1 oz.
Garlic, chopped finely	$\frac{1}{2}$ oz.
Onion, cut into 1 inch pieces	2 ozs.
Pineapple	$\frac{1}{2}$ tin

Seasoning

Sugar	1 teaspoon
Salt	1 teaspoon
Light soy sauce	2 tablespoons
Pepper	$\frac{1}{4}$ teaspoon
Sesame oil	$\frac{1}{4}$ teaspoon
Water	1 tablespoon
Oil	1 tablespoon

Sauce

Strong vinegar	1 tablespoon
Tomato sauce	3 tablespoons
Water or broth	$\frac{3}{4}$ cup
Cornstarch	1 tablespoon
Tomato purée	1 tablespoon
Sugar	3 tablespoons

PROCEDURE

1. Marinate pork cubes with seasoning. Stand for ten minutes.

2. Break an egg over pork and mix well and roll each piece of meat in cornstarch.

3. Fry in deep oil until light brown, take it out with a strainer, drain and fry again, then put aside.

4. Stir fry ginger, onions and garlic in 2 tablespoons oil, add pepper, pour sauce over it and cook till it thickens.

5. Pour the above sauce and ingredients over the pork pieces. Then add the pineapple, garnish with parsley and it is ready to serve.

Variation: Spare ribs and fish can also be pre-prepared in this manner.

Servings: Four

BEEF FILLET WITH TARO
香芋牛柳

Ingredients

*Taro, steamed and sliced	8 ozs.
Beef fillet, sliced	8 ozs.
Spring onion	2 stalks
Root ginger	2 pieces
Water	1 tablespoon
Bicarbonate of soda	$\frac{1}{2}$ teaspoon

Seasoning

Dark soy sauce	2 tablespoons
Cornstarch	1 tablespoon
Sesame oil	$\frac{1}{2}$ teaspoon
Pepper	$\frac{1}{4}$ teaspoon
Sugar	$\frac{1}{2}$ teaspoon
Oil	1 tablespoon
Water	$\frac{1}{2}$ tablespoon

Sauce

Evaporated milk	$\frac{1}{4}$ cup
Water	$\frac{1}{2}$ cup
Chicken cube or	1 cube
Monosodium glutamate	1 teaspoon
Salt	1 teaspoon
Sesame oil	$\frac{1}{2}$ teaspoon
Cornstarch	$\frac{1}{4}$ tablespoon

PROCEDURE

1. Steam taro until soft and slice into pieces.

2. Slice beef into thin pieces and season with the above seasoning. Let stand for 1 hour.

3. Heat 2 tablespoons oil, brown spring onions and root ginger, stir fry beef and pour over taro.

4. Cook sauce mixture and bring to boil. Then pour on top of beef, ready to serve.

To serve: Put taro and beef into an earthware pot for a perfect winter meal.

Servings: Four to Six

*Sweet potato.

LIVER WITH GINGER SAUCE

薑葱豬潤

Ingredients

Liver, sliced 2″ pieces	6 ozs.
Pork fillet, sliced	4 ozs.
Root ginger, shredded	1 oz.
Spring onion, shredded	1 oz.

Seasoning

Cornstarch	1 tablespoon
Salt	1 tablespoon
Sesame oil	1 teaspoon

PROCEDURE

1. Clean liver and rub dry. Slice and season with the above seasoning.
2. Heat 4 cups boiling water, add 1 chopped chicken cube. Blanch pork slices and liver for 2 minutes.
3. Add shredded ginger and spring onions on top of liver and sprinkle 2 tablespoons hot oil, 1 tablespoon dark soy sauce, 1 tablespoon light soy sauce and $\frac{1}{4}$ teaspoon pepper and it is ready to serve.

Variation: Cooked lettuce can be added but liver should be placed on top of lettuce.

Servings: Four

FRIED PORK WITH VEGETABLES

時菜肉片

Ingredients

*Pak Choy, seasonal vegetable	10 ozs.
Lean pork fillet, sliced	8 ozs.
Spring onion, cut into sections	2 stalks
Root ginger, shredded	1 piece

Seasoning

Light soy sauce	1 tablespoon
Sesame oil	1 teaspoon
Cornstarch	1 tablespoon
Pepper	$\frac{1}{4}$ teaspoon
Oil, cooked	1 tablespoon
Water	1 tablespoon

Sauce

Water	$\frac{1}{4}$ cup
Cornstarch	1 teaspoon
Sesame oil	$\frac{1}{4}$ teaspoon
Chicken cube chopped, or monosodium glutamate, 1 teaspoon	

PROCEDURE

1. Heat 5 cups boiling water. Add 1 tablespoon salt, 2 tablespoons oil, a pinch of cooking soda and cook vegetable for 3 minutes. Drain and arrange on both sides of the plate.
2. Heat 3 tablespoons oil in wok or skillet. Add spring onions then stir fry lean pork pieces for 2–3 minutes (high heat). Add sauce, mix well and remove to centre of plate, ready to serve.

Servings: Four to Six
*Chinese cabbage.

PORK PIECES WITH CHILLI SAUCE

回鍋肉片

Ingredients

Lean pork, sliced	8 ozs.
Pepper, cut into triangular pieces	3 ozs.
Red pepper, cut into triangular piece	$\frac{1}{2}$ oz.
Bamboo shoot, sliced	2 ozs.
Leek or spring onion	4 stalks
Ginger	2 pieces
Soy bean paste	$1\frac{1}{2}$ tablespoon

Seasoning

Light soy sauce	2 tablespoon
Cornstarch	1 tablespoon
Pepper	$\frac{1}{4}$ teaspoon
Sesame oil	$\frac{1}{4}$ teaspoon
Sugar	1 teaspoon
Water	1 tablespoon
Oil	1 tablespoon

Sauce

Soy bean paste, fried in oil	1 tablespoon
Garlic, chopped	1 teaspoon
Wine	1 tablespoon
Light soy sauce	1 tablespoon
Sugar	1 tablespoon
Sesame oil	$\frac{1}{2}$ teaspoon
Water	$\frac{1}{4}$ cup
Cornstarch	1 teaspoon
Shanghai chilli sauce	1 teaspoon

PROCEDURE

1. Season lean pork pieces with seasoning and let stand for 10 minutes.
2. Heat 2 tablespoons oil. Stir-fry green peppers and bamboo shoots, remove to a plate.
3. Heat 2 tablespoons oil. Add garlic, leeks and soy bean paste. Fry lean pork slices for 3 minutes. To serve add sauce and red peppers.

Servings: Four

PORK CHOPS WITH BLACK BEAN SAUCE

豉椒肉排

Ingredients

Pork chops, cut into 1″ pieces	10 ozs.
Onion, chopped	3 ozs.
Red chilli, chopped	$\frac{1}{2}$ ozs.
Green pepper	1 oz.
Spring onion, chopped	3 stalks
Garlic, chopped	1 teaspoon
Ginger, chopped finely	1 teaspoon
Black bean	3 tablespoons

Seasoning

Light soy sauce	$1\frac{1}{2}$ tablespoon
Cornstarch	1 tablespoon
Sesame oil	$\frac{1}{4}$ teaspoon
Sugar	1 teaspoon
Salt	$\frac{1}{2}$ teaspoon
Water	1 tablespoon
Oil	1 tablespoon
Pepper	$\frac{1}{4}$ teaspoon

Sauce

Water, or broth	$\frac{1}{2}$ cup
Chicken cube, crushed	$\frac{1}{2}$ pices
Black bean	2 tablespoon
Cornstarch, use later	1 teaspoon
Garlic	1 teaspoon

PROCEDURE

1. Cut pork chops into 1″ pieces and dry with a towel. Season with the above seasoning and allow to soak for 10 minutes.

2. Put black beans in a bowl and steam over boiling water for 3–4 minutes. Mix well with 2 tablespoons sugar and 2 tablespoons oil.

3. Heat 2 tablespoons oil and stir fry onions, green peppers and carrots for 1 minute, then remove to a plate.

4. Heat 4 tablespoons oil, brown garlic and stir fry pork chops for 5 minutes. Add black beans and sauce after 3–4 minutes. Add the above cooked ingredients and cornstarch, and it is ready to serve.

Servings: Four

PORK CUBES WITH WALNUT

合桃肉丁

Ingredients

Pork fillet, cut into cubes	6 ozs.
Bamboo, cut into cubes	2 ozs.
Walnut	4 ozs.
Celery or carrot, cubes	2 ozs.
Mushroom, cubes soaked	2 pieces

Seasoning

Light soy sauce	$\frac{1}{2}$ tablespoon
Salt	$\frac{1}{2}$ teaspoon
Cornstarch	1 tablespoon
Sesame oil	$\frac{1}{4}$ teaspoon
Pepper	$\frac{1}{4}$ teaspoon
Water	1 tablespoon
Oil	1 tablespoon

Sauce

Water	2 tablespoons
Cornstarch	$\frac{1}{2}$ teaspoon
Sesame oil	$\frac{1}{4}$ teaspoon
Monosodium glutamate	$\frac{1}{2}$ teaspoon

PROCEDURE

1. Cook walnuts in boiling water for 3 minutes., then drain and deep fry in 3 cups hot oil until golden brown and drain again.

2. Season pork cubes with the above seasoning, and let it soak for 10 minutes.

3. Heat 2 tablespoons oil, stir fry bamboo cubes, celery, carrots and mushrooms. Add 1 teaspoon salt and 1 teaspoon wine, mix well and remove to a plate.

4. Heat 3 tablespoons oil, brown spring onions, and stir fry pork cubes for 2–3 minutes. Add the other ingredients together with salt and mix well with walnuts. (Better results can be obtained if pork is fried in oil first.)

Variation: Fried rice noodles can be added and placed at the bottom of the plate.

Servings: Four to Six

SHREDDED PORK WITH SWEET BEAN PASTE (Peking)

京醬肉絲

Ingredients

Pork loin	12 ozs.
Sweet bean paste	1½ tablespoons
Spring onions, shredded	6 stalks
Oil for cooking	

Seasoning

Light soy sauce	1 tablespoon
Cornstarch	1 tablespoon
Wine	1 teaspoon
Water	2 tablespoons
Pepper	¼ teaspoon
Oil	1 tablespoon

Sauce

Sweet bean paste	1½ tablespoons
Wine	1 tablespoon
Sugar	1 teaspoon
Monosodium glutamate	½ teaspoon

PROCEDURE

1. Cut pork loin into 2″ shredded pieces and marinate with seasoning. Let stand for 15 minutes.
2. Heat 3 cups oil and quickly deep-fry shredded pork over medium heat until the colour changes. Remove from stove and drain.
3. Remove all oil except for 2 tablespoons from pan or wok. Stir-fry the sweet bean paste mixture until fragrant. Mix well with the shredded pork, add 1 more tablespoon oil and toss the mixture well.
4. Place shredded onions on plate and place pork on the shredded onions and serve.

Servings: Four to Five

CRISPY PORK SLICES (Peking)

炸里肌肉

Ingredients

Pork loin	12 ozs.
Egg whites	2
Szechuan Peppercorn and salt	1 tablespoon
Oil for cooking	

Seasoning

Wine, or sherry	1 tablespoon
Salt	1 teaspoon

Coating mixture

Egg whites	2
Cornstarch	3 tablespoons

PROCEDURE

1. Cut pork loin into slices (⅓″ thick) and lightly pound them with the blunt edge of cleaver. Then marinate in seasoning and stand for 15 minutes.
2. Beat egg whites together with cornstarch until stiff and coat the pork slices with the egg white mixture.
3. Heat 4–5 cups oil and deep fry pork loin for 1–2 minutes. Drain and place slices on a serving plate. Serve with peppercorn and salt.

Servings: Four to Five

HAM SLICES WITH GARLIC SAUCE (Szechuan)

回鍋肉片

Ingredients

Fresh ham	1 lb.
Spring onions	2 stalks
Root ginger	2 slices
Garlic	3 cloves
Hot chilli or sesame oil	1 tablespoon

For cooking ham

Root ginger	2 slices
Spring onions	2 stalks
Wine, or sherry	2 tablespoons

Sauce

Garlic, chopped finely	3 cloves
Sugar	1 teaspoon
Dark vinegar	1 tablespoon
Dark soy sauce	2 tablespoons
Monosodium glutamate	½ teaspoon
Hot chilli oil or chopped fresh chilli	1 tablespoon

PROCEDURE

1. Cook ham in sufficient water to cover, together with ginger, spring onions and wine. Bring to the boil and simmer for ½ hour. Remove from stove and drain.
2. Cut ham into thin bite-size slices and rinse with boiling water and drain. Arrange on a serving plate.
3. Pour sauce over ham slices and garnish with parsley.

Servings: Four to Five

STEWED LION'S HEAD IN POT
紅燒獅子頭

Ingredients

Lean pork, chopped and minced	16 ozs.
Tientsin cabbage, chopped in 2″ sections or Chinese cabbage	8 ozs.
Spring onion	4 stalks
Dried mushroom, shredded	4 pieces
Root ginger	2 pieces
Vermicelli	$\frac{1}{4}$ oz.

Seasoning

Light soy sauce	2 tablespoons
Cornstarch	$\frac{1}{2}$ tablespoon
Salt	$\frac{1}{2}$ teaspoon
Monosodium glutamate	$\frac{1}{2}$ teaspoon
Ginger juice	1 teaspoon
Pepper	$\frac{1}{8}$ teaspoon
Sesame oil	$\frac{1}{8}$ teaspoon

Oil	1 tablespoon

Sauce

Chicken broth	3 cups
Cornstarch	3 tablespoons
Dark soy sauce	1 tablespoon

PROCEDURE

1. Mix chopped lean pork with the above seasoning, and make into 4 meat balls. Rub with cornstarch, deep fry in 4 cups oil, drain.
2. Heat 2 tablespoons oil, brown ginger and spring onions and cook cabbage in 3 cups broth for 10 minutes. Add 4 meat balls, mushrooms, and vermicelli and cook for 5 minutes.
3. Uncover and thicken with sauce, ready to serve.

Servings: Four

ROAST PORK (Chinese Style)
甘香叉燒

Ingredients

Pork shoulder	$1\frac{1}{2}$ lb.

Seasoning

Light soy sauce	2 tablespoons
Sugar	1 tablespoon
Soy bean paste	1 tablespoon
Plum sauce	2 tablespoons
Oil	1 tablespoon
*Rose wine	2 tablespoons
Sesame paste, optional	1 teaspoon
Salt	$\frac{1}{2}$ teaspoon
Monosodium glutamate	$\frac{1}{2}$ teaspoon
Shallot, chopped finely	1 clove
Garlic, chopped finely	1 clove
Sesame oil	1 teaspoon
Honey	1 tablespoon

PROCEDURE

1. Wash pork and rub dry. Cut into strips, 6″ × 3″ × $2\frac{1}{2}$″.
2. Combine seasoning. Marinate with pork for 1 hour.
3. Place strips of pork over rack and roast for about 25 minutes (475°F, Gas 9)
4. Brush pork strips with honey and seasame oil and roast a further 10 minutes at slightly lower temperature.
5. Cut roast pork into big slices and garnish with pineapple and tomato or fried shrimp pieces.

Servings: Six
*See glossary. Brandy or dry sherry may be substituted.

SPECIAL PORK CHOP
京都排骨

Ingredients

Pork chop	16 ozs.
Pineapple	4 pieces
Tomato	2
Parsley	1 oz.

Seasoning

Light soy sauce	1 tablespoon
Dark soy sauce	1 tablespoon
Wine	1 tablespoon
Cornstarch	$\frac{1}{2}$ tablespoon
Pepper	1 teaspoon
Sugar	1 tablespoon
Garlic, chopped	1 tablespoon

Sauce

Worcestershire sauce	1 tablespoon
Sugar	2 tablespoons
Wine	1 teaspoon
Garlic, chopped finely	$\frac{1}{2}$–1 tablespoon

PROCEDURE

1. Cut pork chops into $1\frac{1}{2}$″ pieces and season as above.
2. Deep fry pork chops in 5 cups hot oil twice until it is golden brown, drain and remove to a plate.
3. Clean pan or wok and heat oil (1 tablespoon), brown garlic, add pork chops and mix together with the sauce mixture. Remove to a plate.
4. Garnish with parsley, pineapple, tomato slices, and serve.

Servings: Four and Six

Seafood
海鮮類

Chinese eat a lot of seafood

and as a result Chinese seafood cuisine has been developed

to a very high standard.

Generally fish like Bream and Schnapper

are more suitable for Chinese recipes

as they do not have a distinctive fish taste.

Many of the recipes in this section use Garoupa

which is a fish common in waters around

the Chinese mainland.

However, Bream, Schnapper, and similar fish

are satisfactory substitutes in most of these recipes.

A point worth mentioning is to check for freshness when buying fish.

Fresh fish usually have bulging clear eyes while

those not so fresh have sunken red eyes.

ASSORTED SEA FOOD SUPREME

串燒海上鮮

Ingredients

Garoupa or other fish, cubed	12 ozs.
Prawns, shelled	12 ozs.
Green chilli	8 pieces
Onion	8 ozs.
Oil for cooking	

Seasoning

Shallot	1 tablespoon
Light soy sauce	1 tablespoon
Salt	$\frac{1}{2}$ tablespoon
Pepper	$\frac{1}{2}$ teaspoon
Sesame oil	$\frac{1}{2}$ teaspoon
Water	$\frac{1}{2}$ tablespoon
Oil	$\frac{1}{2}$ tablespoon

Sauce

Tomato ketchup	4 tablespoons
Water	2 tablespoons
Light soy sauce	1 teaspoon
Dark vinegar	1 tablespoon
Garlic, chopped	$\frac{1}{2}$ teaspoon
Sugar	1 tablespoon
Chilli sauce	1 teaspoon
Sesame oil	1 teaspoon
Oil	1 tablespoon

PROCEDURE

1. Marinate fish and prawns in seasoning for $\frac{1}{2}$ hour.
2. Put fish cubes, onions and green chilli on a Satay stick.
3. Heat 5 cups of oil and deep fry the above on medium heat for 5 minutes.
4. Drain and serve with the sauce. Garnish with pineapple and tomatoes.

Servings: Six to Seven

GAROUPA FILLET WITH CELERY

芹菜班球

Ingredients

Garoupa or other fish fillet	10 ozs.
Celery, cut into sections and parboil	4–5 ozs.
Carrots, sliced and parboil	3 ozs.
Root ginger, shredded	2 pieces
Spring onion, cut into sections	2 stalks
Garlic, chopped fine	$\frac{1}{4}$ teaspoon

Seasoning

Salt	1 teaspoon
Sesame oil	$\frac{1}{2}$ teaspoon
Pepper	$\frac{1}{4}$ teaspoon
Ginger juice	1 teaspoon
Water	$\frac{1}{2}$ tablespoon
Oil	$\frac{1}{2}$ tablespoon

Sauce

Chicken broth or water	3 tablespoons
Sesame oil	a few drops
Cornstarch	1 tablespoon

PROCEDURE

1. Clean fish fillet and rub dry with towel, cut into 1″ × 1″ cubes and marinate with the seasoning and let stand for 15 minutes.
2. Heat 3 cups oil in wok and quickly deep fry fish cubes for 2 minutes. Drain and remove to a plate.
3. Heat $1\frac{1}{2}$ tablespoons oil in wok, add celery, garlic, root ginger and spring onions. Toss well, add sauce and serve, after mixing well with fish cubes. Garnish with parsley.

Servings: Four

FRIED GAROUPA ON TOAST

鍋貼石班

Ingredients

Garoupa or other fish fillet	1 lb.
Bread, remove crust and slice	6 slices
Parsley	1 oz.
Eggs, beaten	2

Seasoning

Sesame oil	$\frac{1}{4}$ teaspoon
Eggs, beaten	2
Pepper	$\frac{1}{4}$ teaspoon
Salt	2 teaspoons

PROCEDURE

1. Clean and dry fish fillet, then cut into slices, $2\frac{1}{2}″ × 1\frac{1}{2}″$ and marinate in seasoning.
2. Spread each piece of bread with a piece of the seasoned fish.
Heat 5 cups oil, (high heat) and gently drop in bread (medium heat) and fry until golden brown.
3. Drain on absorbent paper, garnish with parsley, and serve hot.

Servings: Four to Six

RED COOKED FISH FILLET

紅燒班球

Ingredients

Fish fillet, cod, halibut, or haddock	12 ozs.
Root ginger, shredded	1 piece
Spring onion, dropped	2 stalks
Oil for cooking	

Seasoning

Light soy sauce	1 tablespoon
Salt	$\frac{1}{2}$ teaspoon
Sesame oil	$\frac{1}{4}$ teaspoon
Pepper	$\frac{1}{5}$ teaspoon
Water	$\frac{1}{2}$ tablespoon
Oil	$\frac{1}{2}$ tablespoon

Batter

Flour	$\frac{1}{2}$ cup
Cornstarch	2 tablespoons
Baking powder	1 teaspoon
Oil	$\frac{1}{2}$ teaspoon
Water, enough water to make mixture runny	

Sauce

Chicken broth	4 tablespoons
Cornstarch	1 teaspoon
Dark soy sauce	1 teaspoon
Root ginger, shredded	2 pieces
Spring onions, chopped	2 stalks

PROCEDURE

1. Cut fish into 2″ cubes. Cover well with, seasoning.

2. Heat boiling oil and dip fish cubes in batter and deep fry until crispy. Drain and remove to the plate.

3. Heat 2 tablespoons oil, brown spring onions and ginger. Add sauce and bring to boil. Pour over fish and serve.

Servings: Three

CRISPY GAROUPA WITH LEMON SAUCE

檸汁脆皮石班球

Ingreidents

Garoupa or other fish fillet	10 ozs.
Red chilli, cubed	1
Green chilli, cubed	2
Lemon, juice	4 tablespoons

Seasoning

Pepper	$\frac{1}{4}$ teaspoon
Salt	1 teaspoon
Sesame oil	$\frac{1}{2}$ teaspoon
Monosodium glutamate	$\frac{1}{4}$ teaspoon
Ginger juice	1 teaspoon

Batter

Flour	1 cup
Baking powder	$1\frac{1}{2}$ teaspoon
Cornstarch	4 tablespoons
Oil	1 tablespoons
Water, enough to make runny	

Sauce

Water	1 cup
Cornstarch	1 tablespoon
Lemon, Juice	4 tablespoons
Sugar	2–3 tablespoons
Light soy sauce	1 teaspoon
Salt	$\frac{1}{4}$ teaspoon
Monosodium glutamate	1 teaspoon

PROCEDURE

1. Marinate fish in seasoning, let stand for 10 minutes and mix well with batter.

2. Heat oil (4–5 cups) and deep fry fish cubes until golden brown, drain and remove to a serving plate.

3. Heat 2 tablespoons oil, brown 1 teaspoon shallots, red and green chilli. Add sauce and lemon juice, pour over fish cubes and serve. Garnish with parsley.

Servings: Four

FISH AND MUSHROOMS

雜錦會魚中

Ingredients

Seasonal fish	1 lb.
*Rice sheets or bean curd sheet, cut into 2" × 1" pieces	½ lb.
Bamboo shoot, sliced	2 ozs.
Mushroom, sliced	4 pieces
Lean pork, sliced	2 ozs.
Spring onion, chopped	2 stalks
Root ginger, shredded	2 pieces
Salt	

Seasoning

(mushrooms)

Wine	1 teaspoon
Sugar	½ teaspoon

Seasoning

(pork)

Cornstarch	½ teaspoon
Light soy sauce	½ teaspoon

Sauce

Chicken broth or water	1½ cup
Dark soy sauce	1 tablespoon
Cornstarch	1 tablespoon
Sesame oil	½ teaspoon
Chicken cube, or 1 teaspoon Monosodium glutamate	1

PROCEDURE

1. Season fish with salt and lightly fry with 2 tablespoons oil.

2. Heat pot with 2 tablespoons oil. Stir fry ginger, spring onions, mushrooms and lean pork. Pour in sauce and cook for 5 minutes.

3. Put in rice sheets and fish on top, cover and cook for another 5 minutes.

Variation: Two ounces of seasonal vegetable may be added.

Servings: Four to Six

*Obtainable at Chinese delicatessen.

ASSORTED SEAFOOD

海鮮大會

Ingredients

Garoupaor other fish fillet, sliced 2" × 1½" × ½"	4 ozs.
Prawn, shelled	6 ozs.
Squid, cut into pieces	4 ozs.
Eggplant, sliced	2 ozs.

Seasoning

(for Garoupa)

Salt	½ teaspoon
Pepper	¼ teaspoon
Sesame oil	½ teaspoon

(for Prawn) same as above

(for Squid)

Salt	1 pinch
Bicarbonate of soda	1 pinch
Sesame oil	¼ teaspoon
Pepper	¼ teaspoon

Batter

Flour	1 cup
Cornstarch	4 tablespoons
Bicarbonate of soda	1 teaspoon
Oil	1 teaspoon
Water, enough for a running consistency	

PROCEDURE

1. Cut garoupa fillet into pieces and season with the above seasoning, then dip in batter and deep fry until golden brown. Drain.

2. Shell prawns, remove black vein and cut into halves, leaving the tail. Season and deep fry in hot oil until brown.

3. Clean squid and then season with the above seasoning. Dip in batter and deep fry in oil until golden brown.

4. (a) Cut eggplant into thin pieces ¼". Dip in batter and deep fry in hot oil until crispy.

    (b) Cut onion and pepper rings and garnish round the plate of seafood.

5. Stir fry 1 tablespoon salt and 1 teaspoon five spice power for 1 minute. Use as a dip.

Servings: Six to Eight

ASSORTED FISH IN POT

雜錦會黃魚

Ingredients

Seasonal fish	12 ozs.
Turnips, sliced and cooked	10 ozs.
Carrots, sliced and cooked	2 ozs.
Ham, sliced	4 ozs.
Mushrooms, soaked and seasoned with wine and sugar	8 pieces
Spring onion	4 stalks
Root ginger	2 pieces

Seasoning

Bean paste	3 tablespoons
Salt	$\frac{1}{2}$ tablespoon
Wine	1 teaspoon
Cornstarch	1 tablespoon
Pepper	$\frac{1}{4}$ teaspoon

Sauce

Light soy sauce	2 tablespoons
Water	$2\frac{1}{2}$ cups
Chicken cube	1
Sesame oil	1 teaspoon
Cornstarch, use later	1 tablespoon

PROCEDURE

1. Marinate fish in seasoning and stand for 10 minutes. Deep fry until golden brown.
2. Heat 2 tablespoons oil, brown ginger, spring onions and bean paste and stir fry carrots and turnips. Add sauce and fish. Cook for 10 minutes. Thicken with cornstarch and serve in pot.

Servings: Five to Six

SHARK'S FIN WITH EGGS

炒桂花翅

Ingredients

Eggs, beaten	8 eggs
Shark's fin, ready-cooked	8 ozs.
*Silver sprout	4 ozs.
*Chinese ham, shredded	1 oz.
Chives, cut into sections	2 ozs.
Parsley	1 oz.
Ham, chopped	1 oz.

For shark's fin

Water	2 cups
Root ginger	1 piece
Spring onion	2 stalks
Oil	2 tablespoons
Chicken cube	1 piece

PROCEDURE

1. In a bowl add chives and 1 teaspoon salt to beaten eggs.
2. Fry silver sprouts with a pinch of salt and a piece of ginger.
3. Cook ready-cured shark's fin with 2 cups water, together with 2 tablespoons oil, ginger, spring onions and 1 chicken cube. Let simmer for 15 minutes, drain and add to beaten egg mixture.
4. Heat 4–5 tablespoons oil, fry egg mixture, add silver sprouts. After 1 minute, remove to a serving plate, sprinkle ham on top and garnish with parsley.

Servings: Four to Six
*See glossary.

CRACKLING RICE WITH SHRIMP SAUCE

蝦仁鍋巴

Ingredients

Prawn, medium size, shelled	10 ozs.
Crackling rice pieces, obtainable in Chinese grocery stores	6 ozs.
Onion, cubed	4 ozs.
Green peas	3 ozs.
Tomatos, cubed	2 ozs.
Root ginger	1 piece
Spring onion, chopped	
Oil for cooking	

Seasoning

Salt	1 teaspoon
Cornstarch	$\frac{1}{2}$ teaspoon
Pepper	$\frac{1}{4}$ teaspoon
Sesame oil	$\frac{1}{4}$ teaspoon

Sauce

Water	1 cup
Tomato sauce	3 tablespoons
Tomato paste	1 teaspoon
Vinegar	1 tablespoon
Sugar	3 tablespoons
Cornstarch	1 tablespoon
Red chilli	1 teaspoon
Garlic, chopped	1 teaspoon

PROCEDURE

1. Marinate prawns in seasoning. Let stand for 10 minutes.
2. Heat 3 tablespoons oil, brown ginger, garlic, spring onions, onions and tomatoes. Stir fry prawns and add sauce. Then add green peas and chilli, and remove to a big bowl.
3. Heat 4 cups oil and deep fry rice pieces until light brown. Drain and remove to a plate. Serve with shrimp sauce.

Servings: Four to Five

SLICED GAROUPA FILLET IN WINE SAUCE

白酒石班片

Ingredients

Garoupa or other fish fillet, sliced	12 ozs.
Dried mushroom, quartered	6 pieces
Egg white	1 egg
*Cloud ear	6 pieces
Root ginger, shredded	3 pieces
Spring onion, shredded	4 stalks

Seasoning

Cornstarch, use later	1½ tablespoon
Salt	½ teaspoon
Pepper	¼ teaspoon
Egg White	1 egg
Oil	1 tablespoon
Water	1 tablespoon

Sauce

Water or soup stock	1 cup
Chinese white wine or dry sherry	2 tablespoons
Sugar	1 teaspoon
Cornstarch	1 tablespoon
Salt	½ teaspoon

PROCEDURE

1. Soak mushrooms in warm water for ½ hour drain, and discard hard stems, then cut into quarters.
2. Soak cloud ears in water for ½ hour and wash in running water.
3. Season fish fillet with the above seasoning and mix well with cornstarch.
4. Heat 3 cups of oil and quick fry fish slices for a minute (half cook), drain, then remove fish slices to a plate.
5. Heat 1 tablespoon oil, add ginger, spring onions, mushrooms, and cloud ears. Fry a little, add sauce, bring to boil and cook together with fish slices for 1 minutes. To serve, garnish with spring onions.

Servings: Four
*See glossary.

SMOKED FISH

五彩煙鱠魚

Ingredients

Seasonal fish	1½ lb.
Onion, chopped finely	1
Tomato, sliced	2
Pineapple, sliced	1 tin
Tea leaves	3 tablespoons
Sugar, crushed	2 cubes

Seasoning

Wine	1 tablespoon
Dark soy sauce	2 tablespoons
Pepper	¼ teaspoon
Salt	1 teaspoon
Monosodium glutamate	½ teaspoon
Shallots	1 teaspoon

Sauce

Light soy sauce	2–3 tablespoons
Sesame oil	1 teaspoon

PROCEDURE

1. Clean fish and rub dry, slice into 1″ pieces and marinate in seasoning. Allow to stand for 15 minutes.
2. Deep fry fish until it is golden brown. Drain and put aside.
3. Put aluminum foil on bottom of pan together with tea leaves and sugar. Place fish on a wire stand over high heat and smoke for 5 minutes. Remove to a plate.
4. Garnish with pineapple, tomatoes and parsley and serve with sauce.

Servings: Four to Six

Garoupa Fillet with Celery ▶
Overpage Left: Crispy Garoupa with Lemon Sauce
Overpage Right: Shrimp Toast with Sesame Seed

GOLDEN FISH

金縷衣

Ingredients

Fish fillet, sliced, fish head, fish tail	2 lbs..
Mushroom, shredded	1 oz.
Root ginger, shredded	5 pieces
Spring onion, shredded	6 stalks
Ham, shredded	2 ozs.
*Butter paper, 4″ × 4″	20 pieces

Seasoning

Light soy sauce	1 tablespoon
Ginger juice	1 teaspoon
Pepper	$\frac{1}{4}$ teaspoon
Cornstarch	1 tablespoon
Sesame oil	1 tablespoon
Water	1 tablespoon
Oil	1 tablespoon

PROCEDURE

1. Rub head and tail of fish with cornstarch and deep fry in 2 cups of oil.
2. Marinate fish slices in seasoning and let stand for 10 minutes.
3. Put 1 piece of fish fillet, mushroom, ginger, spring onion and ham on butter paper and wrap neatly in a package.
4. Heat oil and deep fry fish packages until light golden brown.
5. Arrange fish head and tail on dish and the fish packages in the middle. Garnish with parsley and serve.

Servings: Six
*Greaseproof.

FRIED FISH WITH BLACK BEAN SAUCE

豉椒魚球

Ingredients

Fish, Mackerel or other	16 ozs.
Red chilli, chopped	2 ozs.
Green pepper, chopped	3 ozs.
Spring onion, chopped	2 stalks
Ginger, chopped	1 tablespoon
Onion, chopped	2 ozs.
Chicken cube	1
Oil for cooking	

Seasoning

Salt	$\frac{3}{4}$ tablespoon
Pepper	$\frac{1}{4}$ teaspoon
Cornstarch	$\frac{1}{2}$ teaspoon

Sauce

Black beans	4 tablespoons
Water	$\frac{3}{4}$ cup
Cornstarch	$\frac{3}{4}$ tablespoon

Chicken cube	1
Sesame oil	1 teaspoon
Dark soy sauce	1 teaspoon
Sugar	1 tablespoon
Salt	$\frac{1}{2}$ teaspoon

PROCEDURE

1. Clean fish and rub dry with towel. Marinate in seasoning and let stand for 1 hour.
2. Heat 4–5 tablespoons oil and over medium heat fry fish on both sides until light brown. Drain and remove to a plate.
3. Season black beans with 2 tablespoons oil, 1 tablespoon sugar and steam over boiling water for 3 minutes.
4. Heat 2 tablespoons oil, brown ginger, garlic, peppers, onions and fry black beans. Add sauce. When it thickens, pour over fish and serve.

Servings: Four to Five

FRIED PRAWNS WITH KNOTTED BEAN

長春蝦球

Ingredients

Prawns	16 ozs.
*Long beans	12–16 ozs.
Shallot	2 cloves

Seasoning

Salt	$\frac{1}{2}$ tablespoon
Sesame oil	1 teaspoon
Cornstarch	$\frac{1}{2}$ tablespoon
Egg white	$\frac{1}{2}$ tablespoon
Pepper	$\frac{1}{2}$ teaspoon

Sauce

Water	1 tablespoon
Cornstarch	$\frac{1}{2}$ teaspoon
Sesame oil	$\frac{1}{2}$ teaspoon
Monosodium glutamate	1 pinch

PROCEDURE

1. Clean prawns, shell and keep tail, then dry with a towel. Marinate in seasoning and stand for 10 minutes.
2. Heat 5 cups boiling water. Add 1 tablespoon salt and cook long beans for 2–3 minutes. Drain. Cut into 2 sections and tie into knots.
3. Heat 3–4 tablespoons oil, brown ginger and spring onions, then fry prawns for 2 minutes. Add sauce. When it thickens, remove to centre of a serving plate, surrounded by bean knots and serve.

Servings: Four to Six
*See glossary.

◀ Stewed Crab with Black Beans

FISH FILLET WITH MEAT SAUCE

肉蓉會班球

Ingredients

Fish fillet, cut into big cubes	12 ozs.
Dried mushroom, soaked and shredded	6
Pork fillet, chopped finely	6 ozs.
Egg white	1
Spring onion, shreedded	4 stalks
Ginger, shredded	1 piece
Oil for frying	

Seasoning

(for pork)

Light soy sauce	1 tablespoon
Cornstarch	1 tablespoon
Oil	1 tablespoon
Water	1 tablespoon
Sesame oil	$\frac{1}{4}$ teaspoon
Pepper	$\frac{1}{4}$ teaspoon

(for mushrooms)

Wine	1 tablespoon
Sugar	$\frac{1}{2}$ teaspoon

(for fish fillet)

Light soy sauce	1 tablespoon
Salt	1 teaspoon
Cornstarch	1 tablespoon
Sesame oil	$\frac{1}{2}$ teaspoon
Ginger juice	1 teaspoon
Water	1 tablespoon
Oil	$\frac{1}{2}$ tablespoon

Sauce

Water, or broth	1 cup
Chicken cube, chopped	1
Sesame oil	$\frac{1}{2}$ teaspoon
Sugar	1 teaspoon
Cornstarch	1 tablespoon

PROCEDURE

1. Marinate fish cubes in seasoning.
2. Season mushrooms and pork with individual seasonings.
3. Heat 4 cups of oil, rub fish pieces with cornstarch and deep fry until golden brown. Then put on a plate.
4. Heat oil in a pan or wok, brown ginger and spring onions, and stir fry chopped meat. Pour in sauce, bring to the boil and pour over fish to serve.

Servings: Four to Five

FISH CUBES WITH SWEET & SOUR SAUCE

脆皮石班球

Ingredients

Garoupa or other fish fillet	8–10 ozs.
Red chilli	1 tablespoon
Garlic, chopped	1 teaspoon
Lettuce, shredded for garnishing	4 ozs.
Oil for cooking	

Seasoning

Light soy sauce	2 tablespoons
Salt	$\frac{1}{4}$ teaspoon
Sesame oil	$\frac{1}{2}$ teaspoon
Pepper	$\frac{1}{4}$ teaspoon
Ginger juice	1 teaspoon
Water	1 tablespoon
Oil	1 tablespoon

Batter

Flour	1 cup
Cornstarch	4 tablespoons
Baking powder	$1\frac{1}{2}$ teaspoon
Oil	1 teaspoon
Water, enough to make mixture runny	

Sweet and sour sauce

Water	$\frac{3}{4}$ cup
Tomato sauce	3 tablespoons
Tomato purée	1 tablespoon
Vinegar	2 tablespoons
Sugar	3 tablespoons
Cornstarch	1 tablespoon
Chicken cube	1
Sesame oil	$\frac{1}{4}$ teaspoon
Garlic	1 teaspoon
Red chilli	1 teaspoon

PROCEDURE

1. Cut fish fillet into 1 inch cubes. Marinate in seasoning and stand for 10 minutes
2. Heat wok and add 3 cups of oil. Dip fish in batter and deep fry in hot oil until golden brown. Drain and remove to a plate.
3. Heat 1 tablespoon oil, stir fry garlic, add sweet and sour sauce, bring to the boil, and pour into a bowl.

To serve: Garnish the plate of fish cubes with shredded lettuce and serve sweet and sour sauce as dip.

Servings: Four

FRIED PRAWNS WITH CHILLI SAUCE

辣汁明蝦

Ingredients
Prawns	$1\frac{1}{2}$ lbs.
Onion, shredded	4 ozs.
Pepper, shredded	3 ozs.
Oil for cooking	

Seasoning
Light soy sauce	2 tablespoons
Ginger juice	1 tablespoon
Pepper	$\frac{1}{4}$ teaspoon
Sesame oil	$\frac{1}{4}$ teaspoon
Sugar	1 teaspoon
Salt	$\frac{1}{2}$ teaspoon

Sauce
Water	$\frac{3}{4}$ cup
Honey	2 tablespoons
Chilli	1 teaspoon
Sesame oil	$\frac{1}{2}$ teaspoon
Light soy sauce	1 teaspoon
Cornstarch	$\frac{1}{2}$ tablespoon

PROCEDURE
1. Clean prawns and rub dry. Remove black vein and cut away the feet. Marinate in seasoning, and stand for $\frac{1}{2}$ hour.
2. Heat 5 cups oil. Fry prawns until the colour changes to pink. Drain and remove to a hot plate.
3. Heat 1 tablespoon oil, stir fry onions and peppers for 1 minute. Add sauce and bring to boil. Pour over prawns and serve.

Servings Four to Six

FISH CUBES WITH BROCCOLI

芥蘭班球

Ingredients
Garoupa or other fish fillet	8–10 ozs.
Broccoli	10 ozs.
Spring onion, cut into sections	2 stalks
Root ginger	2 pieces

Seasoning
Cornstarch	1 tablespoon
Wine	1 teaspoon
Sugar	1 teaspoon
Salt	1 teaspoon
Pepper	$\frac{1}{4}$ teaspoon
Sesame oil	$\frac{1}{4}$ teaspoon
Ginger juice	1 teaspoon
Water	1 tablespoon
Oil	$\frac{1}{2}$ tablespoon

Sauce
Broth or water	$\frac{1}{4}$ cup
Sesame oil	4 drops
Cornstarch	$\frac{1}{2}$ teaspoon
Sugar	$\frac{1}{2}$ teaspoon
Salt	$\frac{1}{2}$ teaspoon
Wine	$\frac{1}{2}$ teaspoon
Chicken cube, crushed	$\frac{1}{2}$ cube
Monosodium glutamate	1 teaspoon

PROCEDURE
1. Cut garoupa into cubes and season with the above seasoning.
2. Heat 5 cups of water, add 1 teaspoon sugar, pinch of bicarbonate of soda, 1 big piece ginger, 1 tablespoon wine and cook broccoli for 3 minutes. Drain and remove to a plate.
3. Heat 2 tablespoons oil, brown garlic and fry garoupa cubes. Add sauce, mix well, and it is ready to serve.

Servings: Four

FRIED PRAWN WITH VEGETABLES

雙蔬會蝦球

Ingredients

Prawn	16 ozs.
Cauliflower	8–10 ozs.
Broccoli, chopped	8–10 ozs.
Root ginger, chopped	1 piece
Spring onion, chopped	2 stalks
Oil for cooking	
Garlic	
Chicken cube	
Salt	
Pinch of bicarbonate of soda	

Seasoning

Cornstarch	1 tablespoon
Sesame oil	$\frac{1}{2}$ teaspoon
Salt	1 teaspoon
Egg white	1 tablespoon
Oil	1 teaspoon

Sauce

Water or chicken broth	3 tablespoons
Sesame oil	$\frac{1}{4}$ teaspoon
Cornstarch	$\frac{1}{2}$ teaspoon
Monosodium Glutamate	$\frac{1}{2}$ teaspoon

PROCEDURE

1. Clean prawns with salt. Remove shell and head. Marinate in seasoning and keep in refrigerator for 30 minutes.
2. Heat 2 tablespoons oil, brown garlic and fry cauliflower. Add 1 cup water, chicken cube and cook for 5 minutes. Drain and remove to a plate.
3. Heat 3–4 cups water, add ginger, 2 tablespoon oil, 1 tablespoon salt, bicarbonate of soda and cook green vegetable for 3 minutes. Divided in 4 sections, drain and place on dish.
4. Heat boiling oil and quick fry prawns for 1 minute, drain and stir fry prawns together with ginger and spring onions for another 1 minute.
5. Add sauce, mix well and pour over vegetables to serve.

Servings: Four to Six

SWEET AND SOUR FISH FINGERS

甜酸魚條

Ingredients

Garoupa or other fish fillet	12–16 ozs.
Carrot, shredded	1 cup

Seasoning

Pepper	$\frac{1}{4}$ teaspoon
Ginger juice	$\frac{1}{2}$ tablespoon
Light soy sauce	1 teaspoon
Salt	1 teaspoon
Sesame oil	1 teaspoon
Cornstarch	1 tablespoon
Water	1 tablespoon
Oil	1 tablespoon

Batter

Flour	1 cup
Cornstarch	4 tablespoons
Oil	1 tablespoon
Baking powder	$1\frac{1}{2}$ teaspoon
Water, enough water to make mixture fluid	

Sweet and sour sauce

Water	$\frac{3}{4}$ cup
Tomato sauce	3 tablespoons
Tomato puree	1 tablespoon
Vinegar	1 tablespoon
Sugar	3 tablespoons
Chicken cube	1 cube
Cornstarch	1 tablespoon
Sesame oil	$\frac{1}{2}$ teaspoon
Garlic, chopped fine	1 teaspoon

PROCEDURE

1. Clean fish and rub it dry with a towel and cut into long pieces $\frac{1}{3}'' \times 2\frac{1}{2}'' \times \frac{1}{2}''$. Season with the above seasoning and let soak for 10 minutes.
2. Heat 4–5 cups boiling oil, dip the fish fingers in batter and deep fry in oil until golden brown. Drain and remove to a plate.
3. Heat 1 tablespoon oil, brown garlic and add sauce. When it thickens, add $\frac{1}{2}$ teaspoon red chilli to serve with fish fingers.

Servings: Six

GAROUPA IN CORN SAUCE

粟米石班塊

Ingredients

Garoupa, thick slices 1″	1 lb.
Sweet corn	1 tin
Egg	1 egg
Root ginger and spring onion, shredded	1 tablespoon

Seasoning

Salt	$\frac{1}{2}$ tablespoon
Pepper	$\frac{1}{2}$ tablespoon
Root ginger, shredded	$\frac{1}{4}$ teaspoon
Sesame oil	$\frac{1}{4}$ teaspoon
Cornstarch	1 tablespoon

Sauce

Water	$\frac{1}{2}$ cup
Corn, sweet	1 tin
Egg White	1 tablespoon
Cornstarch	1 tablespoon
Salt	$\frac{1}{2}$ tablespoon
Sesame oil	$\frac{1}{2}$ teaspoon

PROCEDURE

1. Clean fish and rub it dry with a towel. Season with the above seasoning and let stand for 10 minutes.
2. Heat boiling water and steam fish over stand for 5 minutes. Drain.
3. Heat 1 tablespoon oil, brown spring onions, add sauce, bring to boil and pour over of fish.

Servings: Four to Six

FRIED GAROUPA WITH SWEET & SOUR SAUCE

甜酸石班塊

Ingredients

Garoupa, cubed	10 ozs.
Ginger	2 pieces
Spring onion, cut into section	1 stalk
Onion, cut into big pieces	2 ozs.
Red and green chilli, cut into cubes	$\frac{1}{2}$ oz.
Pineapple, cut into cubes	4 ozs.
Garlic, chopped fine	1–2 cloves

Seasoning

Salt	1 teaspoon
Pepper	$\frac{1}{4}$ teaspoon
Sesame oil	$\frac{1}{4}$ teaspoon
Cornstarch, rub	3 tablespoons
Egg white	$\frac{1}{2}$ egg

Sauce

Water	1 cup
Tomato sauce	3 tablespoons
Tomato paste	1 teaspoon
Vinegar	1 tablespoon
Sugar	3 tablespoons
Salt	$\frac{1}{2}$ teaspoon
Chicken cube	1 cube
Cornstarch	$1\frac{1}{4}$ tablespoons
Garlic	1 teaspoon

PROCEDURE

1. Cut garoupa fillet into cubes, and season with the above seasoning. Rub with cornstarch.
2. Heat 6 cups oil and deep fry fish cubes until light brown. Drain and remove to a plate.
3. Heat 2 tablespoons oil and stir fry the other ingredients for 1 minute. Add sauce, bring to boil and pour on top of garoupa cubes, ready to serve.

Sauce may also be used as dip.
Servings: Six

FRIED POMFRET WITH BLACK BEAN SAUCE

豉椒鱠魚球

Ingredients

Pomfret or Mackerel sliced $\frac{1}{2}$″	1 lb.
Preserved black beans	4 tablespoons
Red chilli, chopped	$\frac{1}{2}$ tablespoon
Spring onions	1 tablespoon
Garlic	1 teaspoon
Root ginger	$\frac{1}{2}$ teaspoon
Parsley	$\frac{1}{2}$ oz.
Onion	2 tablespoons

Seasoning

Shallot, chopped	1 tablespoon
Dark soy sauce	$\frac{1}{2}$ tablespoon
Light soy sauce	$\frac{1}{2}$ tablespoon
Salt	1 teaspoon
Sugar	1 teaspoon
Ginger juice	$\frac{1}{2}$ tablespoon
Wine	$\frac{1}{2}$ teaspoon
Pepper	$\frac{1}{4}$ teaspoon

Sauce

Water or chicken broth	1 cup
Chicken cube	1 cube
Black beans	4 tablespoons
Red chilli, use later	$\frac{1}{2}$ tablespoon
Chilli	$\frac{1}{2}$ teaspoon
Garlic, chopped	1 teaspoon
Spring onion	1 tablespoon
Cornstarch	1 tablespoon

PROCEDURE

1. Steam black beans over boiling water for 3 minutes together with 1 tablespoon sugar, 2 tablespoons oil. Put aside.
2. Cut pomfret in $\frac{1}{2}$ in. slices, season with the above seasoning for 1 hour.
3. Deep fry fish in 5 cups boiling oil until golden brown, then arrange on a hot plate.
4. Heat 2 tablespoons oil, brown garlic, spring onions, ginger, add black beans. Stir fry a little, add fish and sauce, bring to boil and pour on top of a plate. Garnish with parsley and chopped chillies.

Variation: On cold days, put warm brandy in a little pot, light a flame with a match over brandy, and pour over fish.

Servings: Four to Six

GAROUPA WITH BLACK BEAN SAUCE

豉椒班球

Ingredients

Garoupa, cut into 1″ cubes	$1\frac{1}{2}$ lbs.
Spring onion, chop finely	4 stalks
Root ginger, chop finely	4 pieces
Black bean, steam for 3 minutes together with oil and sugar	4 tablespoons
Green and red chilli	1 tablespoon
Garlic	1 teaspoon

Seasoning

Light soy sauce	1 tablespoon
Cornstarch	1 tablespoon
Sesame oil	$\frac{1}{2}$ teaspoon
Sugar	$\frac{1}{2}$ teaspoon
Pepper	$\frac{1}{4}$ teaspoon
Salt	$\frac{1}{2}$ teaspoon
Ginger juice	1 teaspoon

Sauce

Water	$\frac{3}{4}$ cup
Cornstarch	1 tablespoon
Sesame oil	$\frac{1}{4}$ teaspoon
Sugar	1 tablespoon
Chicken cube, crushed	1 teaspoon

PROCEDURE

1. Clean garoupa and rub it dry with a towel. Chop head and tail of fish into separate pieces and deep fry in hot oil until golden brown. Remove and arrange attractively on a plate, leaving an empty space in the middle of the dish.
2. Cut the rest of the garoupa into cubes and season with the above seasoning and let it absorb for $\frac{1}{2}$ hour. Quick fry in hot oil for 1 minute and drain.
3. Heat 2 tablespoons oil, brown spring onion, root ginger, green and red chillies and garlic. Fry black beans and fish cubes, add sauce and it is ready to serve.

Servings: Six

FRIED SHRIMPS WITH VEGETABLES

雙蔬蝦球

Ingredients

Prawn, shelled, de-vein	12 ozs.
Broccoli, remove leaves and slice	12 ozs.
Carrots, sliced	2 ozs.
Root ginger, sliced	4 slices
Spring onion, sliced	2 stalks

Seasoning

(for prawn)

Salt	1 teaspoon
Sesame oil	$\frac{1}{2}$ teaspoon
Pepper	$\frac{1}{4}$ teaspoon
Cornstarch	$\frac{1}{2}$ teaspoon
Egg white	$\frac{1}{2}$ teaspoon
Oil	1 tablespoon

Sauce

Water	2 tablespoons
Cornstarch	$\frac{1}{2}$ teaspoon
Sesame oil	$\frac{1}{6}$ teaspoon
Monosodium glutamate	$\frac{1}{6}$ teaspoon

PROCEDURE

1. Clean prawns with salted water, then wash with running water, remove head, shell, leaving the tail. de-vein, then season with the above seasoning and put it in the refrigerator for 30 minutes.
2. Wash broccoli and remove leaves, cut into 1 inch sections and cook in 2 cups boiling water for 3 minutes together with 1 tablespoon oil and 1 teaspoon salt. Drain, then remove to a plate.
3. Heat 4 cups oil, quick fry prawns for 1 minute, drain. Pour away all the oil, leaving 2 tablespoons in the wok. Stir fry ginger, spring onions, carrots, broccoli and prawns. Add sauce, mix well, and it is ready to serve.

Servings: Four

DRIED PEPPER PRAWNS

椒鹽大蝦

Ingredients

Prawns	1 lb.

Seasoning

Salt	1 tablespoon
Ginger juice	1 tablespoon
Wine	1 tablespoon
Sesame oil	$\frac{1}{2}$ teaspoon
Pepper	$\frac{1}{2}$ teaspoon
Monosodium glutamate	$\frac{1}{2}$ teaspoon
Cornstarch, use later	2 tablespoons

PROCEDURE

1. Wash and clean prawns with salt. Remove black vein at the back and feet. Rub dry with a towel. Season with the above seasoning for 10 minutes and rub with cornstarch before deep frying.
2. Heat 4–5 cups boiling oil and deep fry prawns until the colour changes to pink. Drain and remove to a plate. Garnish with parsley and chilli.

Servings: Four to Six

SHRIMP TOAST WITH SESAME SEED

芝麻蝦塊

Ingredients

Shrimp, shelled, mashed	1 lb.
Sesame seed	2 ozs.
Bread, sliced, staled	1 lb.
Tomato, for garnishing	2 pieces
Parsley, for garnishing	$\frac{1}{2}$ oz.

Seasoning

Sesame oil	$\frac{1}{2}$ teaspoon
Pepper	$\frac{1}{4}$ teaspoon
Salt	$\frac{1}{2}$ teaspoon
Cornstarch	1 teaspoon

PROCEDURE

1. Clean prawns, shell and dry with a towel. season with the above seasoning, mix well with a pair of chopsticks and freeze for $\frac{1}{2}$ hour.
2. Put mashed shrimps on bread and sprinkle with sesame seeds.
3. Heat 4 cups oil and deep fry shrimp toast until golden brown. Cut into long slices before serving and garnish with tomato pieces and parsley.

Servings: Six

STEWED CRAB WITH BLACK BEANS

豉椒焗蟹

Ingredients

Crab	1–1½ lb.
Spring onion, cut into sections	4 stalks
Preserved black beans, steamed with oil and sugar for 3 minutes	4 tablespoons
Root ginger	4 pieces
Garlic, chopped	1 tablespoon
Red and green chilli, chopped	1 tablespoon

Seasoning

Light soy sauce	2 tablespoons
Ginger juice	1 tablespoon
Salt	1 teaspoon
Sugar	1 teaspoon
Pepper	½ teaspoon
Sesame oil	1 teaspoon

Sauce

Water	1 cup
Chicken cube	1
Sesame oil	½ teaspoon
Sugar	½ teaspoon
Cornstarch	¾ tablespoon
Dark soy sauce	1 teaspoon

PROCEDURE

1. Clean crab and rub it dry. Cut crab into pieces and season with the above seasoning and allow to stand for 10 minutes.
2. Rub crab pieces with cornstarch and deep fry until golden brown. Drain oil and remove to a plate.
3. Heat 2 tablespoons oil and stir fry together with the other ingredients. Add sauce and mix well with crab, before serving.

Servings: Four to Six

FRIED CRISPY OYSTER

酥炸生蠔

Ingredients

Oysters	1 lb.
Salt	1 teaspoon
Vinegar	½ teaspoon
Ginger juice	1 tablespoon
Pepper	¼ teaspoon
Wine	½ tablespoon
Oil for frying	

Batter

Flour	1 cup
Cornstarch	4 tablespoons
Baking powder	1½ teaspoon
Salt	½ teaspoon
Oil	2 tablespoons
Water, enough to make mixture runny	

Spicy Salt

Salt	2 tablespoons
All spice powder	1 teaspoon

PROCEDURE

1. Rub oyster with salt and wash with water a few times.
2. Mix flour, cornstarch, baking powder and salt together with water. Add 2 tablespoons oil. Mix well again. Let mixture rise for 10 minutes.
3. Boil water, add salt and vinegar. Cook oysters for a few minutes, season with ginger juice and pepper. Rub with batter and deep fry until golden brown. Drain and remove to a plate.
4. To make dip, combine spicy salt ingredients and fry over medium heat. Serve in separate bowl.

Servings: Four

SPICY FRIED PRAWNS (Szechuan)

乾燒明蝦

Ingredients

Large green prawns	1½ lb.
Root ginger, chopped finely	1 tablespoon
Spring onions, chopped finely	1 tablespoon
Oil for deep frying	

Sauce

(A)

Garlic, chopped	1 tablespoon
Root ginger, chopped	1 tablespoon
Spring onion, chopped	1 tablespoon

(B)

Hot bean paste	1 teaspoon
Wine or sherry	1 tablespoon
Tomato ketchup	4 tablespoons

(C)

Water or chicken broth	2 tablespoons
Monosodium glutamate	1 teaspoon
Sugar	3 tablespoons
Salt	1 teaspoon
Cornstarch	½ tablespoon

PROCEDURE

1. Clean, shell and de-vein prawns. Drain.
2. Heat 4 cups oil and deep fry prawns until colour changes to pink. Remove from stove and drain.
3. Leave 2 tablespoons oil in pan and brown sauce (A) until fragrant.
4. Add sauce (B) and stir fry for ½ minute.
5. When mixture begins to boil, add prawns and mix well with sauce (C) to thicken. Coat prawns with sauce, remove to a plate and serve, garnished with parsley.

Servings: Five to Six

Vegetables
蔬菜類

Vegetables are an important part of any Chinese meal.

The common vegetables used in the recipes

in this section are easily obtained and provide

a tasty and nourishing supplement to the meal.

The art of preparing vegetables for Chinese cooking

is to use the minimum cooking necessary so that the vegetables

do not lose either their flavour or texture.

The Chinese have developed the subtle blending

of the flavours of different vegetables

to complement and heighten the flavour

of the food they accompany.

ASSORTED VEGETABLE WITH CRAB SAUCE

蟹扒四蔬

Ingredients

Crab meat	¾ cup
*Mustard green, cooked or seasonal vegetable	4 ozs.
Carrot, cooked	4 ozs.
Cauliflower, cooked with salt	4 ozs.
Asparagus, warm	1 tin

Seasoning

Wine	1 tablespoon
Pepper	¼ tablespoon
Sesame oil	1 teaspoon

Sauce

Egg whites	2
Water	¾ cup
Sesame oil	½ tablespoon
Cornstarch	1 teaspoon

PROCEDURE

1. Steam 2 crabs over boiling water for 10 minutes and extract crab meat. Season with seasoning.
2. Arrange the cooked vegetables on the plate.
3. Heat two tablespoons oil, and brown spring onions. Fry crab meat, add sauce and egg white, and serve over vegetables.
*Broccoli.

Servings: Four

ASSORTED VEGETABLES WITH 'PO KOK' SAUCE

葡汁焗四蔬

Ingredients

Chinese cabbage	12 ozs.
*Mustard green	12 ozs.
Carrot, cooked and cut into 2″ × ½″ sticks	6 ozs.
Asparagus, warmed	1 tin
Mushroom, or fresh	1 tin
Ham, sliced	2 ozs.
Pinch of Bicarbonate of soda	

Seasoning

Wine	1 tablespoon
Sugar	½ teaspoon

Sauce

Water	2 cups
Sesame oil	½ teaspoon
Curry powder	1½ tablespoons
Milk	½ cup
Sugar	½ tablespoon
Shallot	1 tablespoon
Oil	2 tablespoons
Salt	1 tablespoon

PROCEDURE

1. Heat 5 cups of boiling water, add a pinch of bicarbonate of soda and cook green vegetables for 3 minutes. Drain and arrange on a heat-proof dish together with asparagus and carrots.
2. Heat 2 tablespoon oil, stir fry mushrooms and spring onions. Add sauce, bring to the boil and pour over vegetables.
3. Put in hot oven, (400°F Gas 6,) for 15 minutes and serve.

Servings: Five to Six
*Broccoli.

FRESH MUSHROOMS WITH VEGETABLES

冬菇扒生菜

Ingredients

Fresh mushroom	1 lb.
Champignon, drained	½ tin
Lettuce, or seasonal vegetable	1 lb.
Spring onion, chopped	2 stalks
Ginger, shredded	2 pieces

Seasoning

Wine	2 tablespoons
Sugar	1 tablespoon
Monosodium glutamate	1 teaspoon

Sauce

Water	⅓ cup
Oyster sauce, or 1 tablespoon dark soy sauce	2 tablespoons
Wine	1 tablespoon
Sugar	1 teaspoon
Cornstarch	½ tablespoon

PROCEDURE

1. Wash mushrooms with salt water and parboil in water for 2–3 minutes with 1 tablespoon wine and 2 pieces of ginger. Drain.
2. Season mushrooms and champignons with above seasoning and let stand for 10 minutes.
3. Heat 4–5 cups boiling water and cook lettuce (or any vegetable) for ½ minute with 2 tablespoons oil, 1 tablespoon salt and 1 piece ginger. Drain and remove to plate.
4. Heat 2–3 tablespoons oil, stir fry spring onions and ginger for ½ minute. Add mushrooms, champignons, then serve. When thick, pour over vegetables and serve.

Servings: Six

MUSTARD GREEN WITH CRAB SAUCE

金銀菜胆

Ingredients

*Mustard green, or seasonal vegetable	2 lbs.
Baby corn, drained	1 tin
Mushroom, drained	2 tins
Crab meat, steamed, extract meat out	2 crabs
Ham, shredded	2 ozs.
Root ginger	1 piece
Oil for cooking	
Pinch of bicarbonate of soda	
Salt	1 tablespoon
Ginger	1 piece
Wine	1 tablespoon

Seasoning

(for crab)

Sesame oil	$\frac{1}{2}$ teaspoon
Pepper	$\frac{1}{4}$ teaspoon
Salt	1 teaspoon

(for mushroom)

Wine	1 tablespoon
Monosodium glutamate	1 teaspoon
Sugar	$\frac{1}{2}$ teaspoon
Salt	$\frac{1}{2}$ teaspoon

Sauce

(for crab meat)

Water	$\frac{1}{2}$ cup
Cornstarch	$\frac{1}{2}$ tablespoon
Sesame oil	$\frac{1}{2}$ teaspoon
Salt	$\frac{1}{2}$ teaspoon
Egg white	1

PROCEDURE

1. Trim and take hearts of vegetable and cook in 4–5 cups of boiling water together with 2 tablespoons oil, bicarbonate of soda, salt, ginger and wine. After 3 minutes drain and remove to a plate, dividing into 2 portions.
2. Heat 2 tablespoons oil, brown 1 teaspoon garlic and fry baby corn for 1 minute. Add $\frac{3}{4}$ cup water and 1 chicken cube and cook for 3–4 minutes. Drain and arrange side by side with cooked vegetable.
3. Heat 3 tablespoons oil, brown 2 pieces shredded ginger and fry mushrooms and crab meat. Add sauce and when it thickens, place in centre of plate.
4. Sprinkle shredded ham on top of mushrooms and serve.
*Broccoli.

Servings: Six to Eight

STUFFED MUSHROOMS WITH SEASONAL VEGETABLE

時菜釀北菇

Ingredients

Mushroom, soak and remove stem	3–4 ozs.
Shrimp, shell and make shrimp paste or, lean pork	1 lb.
Seasonal vegetable	1 lb.
Oil for cooking	
Pinch of bicarbonate of soda	
Salt	1 tablespoon

Seasoning

(for mushrooms)

Wine	1 tablespoon
Sugar	1 tablespoon
Cornstarch	1 teaspoon
Oil	1 teaspoon

(for shrimps)

Pepper	$\frac{1}{4}$ teaspoon
Salt	1 teaspoon
Egg white	1 teaspoon
Sesame oil	$\frac{1}{2}$ teaspoon

Sauce

Black bean, steamed with sugar and oil for 3 minutes	4 tablespoons
Garlic, chopped	$\frac{1}{2}$ tablespoon
Red chilli	1 teaspoon
Water	1 cup
Spring onion, chopped finely	2 tablespoons
Chicken cube	1
Sesame oil	$\frac{1}{2}$ teaspoon
Dark soy sauce, or oyster sauce	$\frac{1}{2}$ teaspoon
Cornstarch	1 tablespoon

PROCEDURE

1. Marinate mushrooms in seasoning. Then steam over boiling water for 10 minutes and drain.
2. Add seasoning to shrimps. Mix well and freeze for $\frac{1}{2}$ hour.
3. Rub a little cornstarch over mushrooms and stuff well with shrimp paste, then steam over boiling water for 10 minutes.
4. Heat 5 cups boiling water. Add 2 tablespoons oil, bicarbonate of soda and salt and cook seasonal vegetable for 3 minutes. Drain and remove to a plate. Arrange stuffed mushrooms on top of vegetable.
5. Heat 1 tablespoon oil, stir fry garlic, spring onions, root ginger and black beans. Add sauce, bring to the boil. Pour over mushrooms and serve.

Servings: Six

FRIED VEGETABLES
炒油菜

Ingredients
*Choy sum	12 ozs.
Broccoli	12 ozs.
Cabbage, Chinese, or any green vegetable	12 ozs.
Root ginger, shredded	1 piece
Five seasoning powder	1 teaspoon
Salt	$\frac{1}{2}$ teaspoon
Water	$\frac{1}{5}$ cup
Oil for cooking	

PROCEDURE

1. Cut vegetables into 2″ or 3″ sections. Wash and clean, then drain.
2. Heat 2 tablespoons boiling oil, add shredded ginger, fry green vegetable, add salt, seasoning powder and water. Cover lid with them mix well, drain, and serve after 3 minutes.

Servings: Two
*See glossary.

MUSHROOMS WITH SEASONAL VEGETABLE
雙菇扒時菜

Ingredients
Dried mushroom, soak and cut off stem	3 ozs.
Button mushrooms	1 cup
*Tientsin Cabbage, or other vegetable, sectioned	1 piece
Root ginger	1 piece
Spring onions	2 stalks
Oil for frying	

Seasoning
Wine	1 tablespoon
Sugar	1 teaspoon

Sauce
Water	1 cup
Dark soy sauce	1 teaspoon
Chicken cube	1
Salt	1 teaspoon
Sugar	$\frac{1}{2}$ teaspoon
Cornstarch, use later	$1\frac{1}{2}$ tablespoon
Sesame oil	$\frac{1}{2}$ teaspoon

PROCEDURE

1. In a pot, heat 3 tablespoons oil. Add a piece of ginger and stir fry cabbage for a minute. Add a cup of water, a chopped chicken cube and cook until soft.
2. Heat 2 tablespoon oil and fry mushrooms and spring onions for a minute. Add salt and cook for 10 minutes.
3. Thicken with cornstarch and pour over vegetables to serve.

Servings: Five
*See glossary.

FRESH MUSHROOMS WITH VEGETABLE
雙菇扒菜胆

Ingredients
Fresh mushrooms	1 lb.
Champignons, drained	1 tin
Quail eggs, cooked, or dried mushrooms	1 dozen
Lettuce	1 lb.
Spring onion	2 stalks
Root ginger	3 pieces
Oil for cooking	
Salt	1 tablespoon

Seasoning
Wine	2 tablespoons
Sugar	1 tablespoon
Monosodium glutamate	1 teaspoon

Sauce
Water	1 cup
Oyster sauce	2 tablespoons
Wine	1 tablespoon
Sugar	1 teaspoon
Cornstarch	$\frac{3}{4}$ tablespoon

PROCEDURE

1. Wash mushrooms with salt water and parboil in water for 2–3 minutes together with 1 tablespoon wine, and 2 pieces of ginger. Drain.
2. Marinate mushrooms and champignons with seasoning for 10 minutes.
3. Heat 4–5 cups boiling water and cook lettuce for $\frac{1}{2}$ minute together with 2 tablespoons oil and tablespoon salt, also with 1 piece ginger. Drain and remove to a plate.
4. Cook quail eggs for 10 minutes in water and remove shell.
5. Heat 2–3 tablespoons oil, stir fry spring onions and ginger for $\frac{1}{2}$ minute, add mushrooms, champignons and quail eggs, then sauce.
6. When mixture thickens, pour over lettuce and serve.

Servings: Four to Five
*If dried mushroons are being used cook for $\frac{1}{2}$ hour then remove stems.

LETTUCE WITH LIGHT SOY SAUCE

白灼生菜

Ingredients

Lettuce	12 ozs.
Light soy sauce	2 tablespoons
Oil, heated	1 tablespoon
Sesame oil	½ teaspoon
Salt	½ tablespoon

PROCEDURE

1. Heat 3 cups boiling water. Add salt, oil, and lettuce and cook for ½ minute. Drain and place on plate.
2. Sprinkle light soy sauce, cooked oil and sesame oil on top and serve.

Servings: Two

CREAMED CHINESE CABBAGE

奶油津白

Ingredients

Chinese cabbage	1 lb.
Milk	½ cup
Boiled ham	1 tablespoon
Mushroom, small	6 pieces
Chicken broth, or water and monosodium glutamate	1 cup
Oil for cooking	

Sauce

Water or broth	1 cup
Milk	½ cup
Cornstarch	1½ tablespoons
Sesame oil	½ teaspoon

PROCEDURE

1. Cut cabbage into small sections. Cook and bring to boil with 1½ cups water or broth. Cook cabbage until soft, then drain and remove to a plate. Save the left-over broth for the sauce.
2. Heat 1 teaspoon oil. Add sauce and bring to boil. Pour over vegetable. Sprinkle with chopped ham and serve.

Servings: Two to Three

FRIED BAMBOO SHOOTS WITH VEGETABLES

炒雙色筍

Ingredients

Bamboo shoots	1½ lbs.
Spinach	1 lb.
Garlic, chopped	1 teaspoon
Oil for cooking	

Sauce

(for bamboo shoots)

Water	1 tablespoon
Wine	1 teaspoon
Monosodium glutamate	1 teaspoon
Dark soy sauce	2 tablespoons
Sugar	½ teaspoon
Sesame oil	½ teaspoon

Seasoning

(for vegetables)

Salt	1 teaspoon
Monosodium glutamate	1 teaspoon
Water	2 tablespoons

PROCEDURE

1. Cut fresh or tinned bamboo shoots into triangular pieces. Heat 2 tablespoons oil and stir fry bamboo shoots. Then add the sauce and cook for 5 minutes. Drain and place on centre of plate.
2. Heat 3 tablespoons oil, brown garlic, and stir fry spinach for 2–3 minutes. Sprinkle water 2–3 times, mix and stir well for 2–3 minutes.
3. To serve, put bamboo shoots in the centre of a long serving plate and arrange the vegetables on the left and right sides.

Servings: Four

BRAISED TURNIPS WITH CHILLI

柱侯蘿蔔

Ingredients

Turnips	1 lb.
Leek or spring onions, chopped	2 stalks
Chilli	1 tablespoon

Sauce

Water or broth	1¼ cups
Chicken cube, chopped	1
Sugar	1 tablespoon
Salt	1 teaspoon
Sesame oil	¼ teaspoon
Bean paste	1 tablespoon

PROCEDURE

1. Peel and cut turnips into 1″ cubes.
2. Heat 2 tablespoons oil, add leeks or spring onions. Stir fry turnips for 1 minute.
3. Add the above sauce and cook until soft.

Servings: Six

FRIED BAMBOO WITH BEAN PASTE (Szechuan)
甜醬冬筍

Ingredients
Bamboo shoot, pre-cooked	2 cups
Spinach	$\frac{3}{4}$ lb.
Oil for deep frying	

Seasoning
To fry with bamboo shoots
Sweet bean paste	2 tablespoons
Light soy sauce	1 tablespoon
Sugar	1 tablespoon
Monosodium glutamate	1 teaspoon
Wine	1 tablespoon
Sesame oil	$\frac{1}{2}$ teaspoon
Water	$\frac{1}{3}$ cup

FRIED BAMBOO SHOOTS WITH VEGETABLES (Shanghai)
青菜燴冬筍

Ingredients
Bamboo shoot, sliced	6 ozs.
Green vegetable	2 ozs.
Oil for cooking	

Sauce
(A)
Water or stock	$\frac{1}{2}$ cup
Salt	$\frac{1}{2}$ teaspoon
Monosodium glutamate	$\frac{1}{4}$ teaspoon
Sugar	$\frac{1}{4}$ teaspoon

STIR FRIED SZECHUAN EGGPLANT
魚香茄子

Ingredients
Eggplant	1 lb.
Lean pork, chopped	4 ozs.
Oil for cooking	
Garlic, chopped	$\frac{1}{2}$ tablespoon
Water	$\frac{1}{2}$ cup
Chicken cube	1
Hot bean paste	1 tablespoon
Green onions, chopped	2 tablespoons
Root ginger, chopped finely	1 tablespoon
Garlic	1 tablespoon

Sauce
Water	$\frac{3}{4}$ cup
Wine	1 tablespoon
Light soy sauce	1 teaspoon

(for vegetable)
Water	3 cups
Salt	$\frac{1}{2}$ teaspoon
Monosodium glutamate	$\frac{1}{2}$ teaspoon
Oil	2 tablespoons

PROCEDURE
1. Cut bamboo shoots into bite size pieces (cross cut) and quick fry in 3 cups oil until light golden brown. Drain, but leave 3 tablespoons oil in the pan.
2. Mix seasoning ingredients together. Heat oil and stir fry ingredients for 2 minutes. Add bamboo shoots and cook until the liquid is nearly dry, then remove to centre of the plate.
3. Heat boiling water, add salt, monosodium glutamate and oil and cook spinach for 3 minutes. Drain and arrange on both sides of serving plate.

Servings: Four

(B)
Water	1 teaspoon
Cornstarch	1 teaspoon
Cooked oil or melted chicken fat	1 tablespoon

PROCEDURE
1. Trim the leaves from the green vegetable, wash, drain and cut into $\frac{1}{3}''$ pieces.
2. Heat 1 cup oil, quickly fry bamboo shoot slices for 1 minute. Drain and remove to a plate.
3. Re-heat 2 tablespoons oil, fry green vegetables, add sauce (A) and bamboo slices, bring to the boil.
4. Thicken with sauce (B), pour this over bamboo shoot slices and serve.

Servings: Three

Monosodium glutamate	1 teaspoon
Sugar	$\frac{1}{2}$ tablespoon
Cornstarch (use later)	$2\frac{1}{2}$ tablespoon
Water	1 tablespoon

PROCEDURE
1. Cut ends from eggplant and discard. Cut into $2\frac{1}{2}''$ sections. Then cut each section into 4 sticks.
2. Heat 3 tablespoons oil, brown $\frac{1}{2}$ tablespoon garlic and fry eggplant. Add chicken cube and water also $\frac{1}{4}$ teaspoon salt and cook eggplant until soft. Drain and remove to a plate.
3. Season chopped lean pork with $\frac{1}{2}$ teaspoon cornstarch and 1 teaspoon water. Then fry in 2 tablespoons oil until fragrant. Add hot bean paste, spring onions, ginger rice and garlic. Mix well.
4. Add eggplant and thicken with cornstarch mixture and serve.

Servings: Four

BEAN CURD WITH MEAT SAUCE

肉蓉扒豆腐

Ingredients

Bean curd, cut into little squares	6–8 pieces
Lean pork, chopped fine	8 ozs.
Spring onion, chopped fine	4 stalks
Green peas	4 ozs.

Seasoning

Light soy sauce	1 tablespoon
Sugar	$\frac{1}{2}$ teaspoon
Salt	$\frac{1}{2}$ teaspoon
Cornstarch	$\frac{3}{4}$ tablespoon
Sesame oil	$\frac{1}{4}$ teaspoon
Pepper	$\frac{1}{4}$ teaspoon
Water	1 tablespoon
Oil	1 tablespoon

Sauce

Shanghai chilli	1–2 tablespoons
Water	$\frac{1}{2}$ cup
Chicken cube, chopped	1
Cornstarch	$1\frac{1}{2}$ tablespoons
Sesame oil	1 teaspoon

PROCEDURE

1. Season bean curd with $\frac{1}{2}$ tablespoon salt.
2. Heat 2 tablespoons oil and fry chopped spring onions together with bean curd. Sprinkle a little light soy sauce and remove to plate.
3. Heat 2 tablespoons oil and fry lean pork for 2 minutes, stirring constantly.
4. Pour in sauce, mix with bean curd and green peas and serve.

Servings: Four to Six

STUFFED TAU FU SUPREME

蒸釀百花豆腐

Ingredients

Prawn, or shrimp	1 lb.
*Bean curd, Tau Fu	8 pieces
Spring onion, chopped	3 stalks

Seasoning

Pepper	$\frac{1}{4}$ teaspoon
Salt	1 teaspoon
Sesame oil	$\frac{1}{2}$ teaspoon
Cornstarch	$\frac{1}{2}$ tablespoon

Sauce

Dark soy sauce	$\frac{1}{2}$ tablespoon
Light soy sauce	2 tablespoons
Ginger juice	3 tablespoons
Pepper	$\frac{1}{4}$ teaspoon
Sesame oil	$\frac{1}{2}$ teaspoon
Spring onion, chopped	2 tablespoons

PROCEDURE

1. Clean prawns and rub dry with a towel. Remove head and shell, then mash with the blade of chopper. Marinate with the above seasoning, mix well and put in refrigerator for $\frac{1}{2}$ hour.
2. Cut Tau Fu in halves, scrape away a little bean curd in the middle and stuff with prawns or shrimp paste. Arrange on plate.
3. Heat 5 cups boiling water, and steam stuffed bean curd for 10 minutes.
4. Sprinkle chopped onions and pour sauce over to serve. Chopped ham can also be added.

Servings: Four
*See glossary.

BRAISED ASSORTED BEAN CURD

四寶扒豆腐

Ingredients

Bean curd or "TAU FU", sliced and fried	8 pieces
Preserved vegetables	1 tin
Lean pork, sliced	4 ozs.
Bamboo, sliced	2 ozs.
Green peas	2 ozs.
Garlic	1 clove
Oil for cooking	

Seasoning

Light soy sauce	1 teaspoon
Cornstarch	$\frac{1}{2}$ teaspoon
Sesame oil	$\frac{1}{2}$ teaspoon

Sauce

Water	$\frac{1}{2}$ cup
Chicken cube	$\frac{1}{2}$ piece
Chilli	1 teaspoon
Dark soy sauce	$\frac{1}{2}$ teaspoon
Cornstarch	$\frac{1}{2}$ tablespoon
Sesame oil	$\frac{1}{4}$ teaspoon

PROCEDURE

1. Heat boiling oil and deep fry sliced bean curd until golden brown. Drain and remove to a plate.
2. Heat 2 tablespoons oil, fry garlic and lean pork for 1 minute. Add preserved vegetables, bamboo shoots and mix well. Then add sauce.
3. When mixture thickens, add green peas and serve over bean curd.

Servings: Four to Five

Note: Bean curd is made of yellow beans and water. It is full of protein, easy to digest and the price is cheap. Stir fry bean curd cubes with spring onions is a HK$1.00 dish or 20 cents Australian.

FRIED BEAN CURD WITH LO HON SAUCE

羅漢扒豆腐

Ingredients

Bean curd, fried	6–8 pieces
Bamboo, tinned or fresh	2 ozs.
Mushroom, soaked, quarters	8 pieces
Green peas	2 ozs.
*Silver sprout, optional	4 ozs.
*Bean curd ball, parboil 1 minute	6 pieces
*Snow fungus, soaked	$\frac{1}{2}$ oz.
Seasonal vegetable	4–5 pieces
Olive seeds	2 ozs.

Seasoning

(*for mushrooms*)

Wine	1 tablespoon
Sugar	$\frac{1}{4}$ teaspoon

Sauce

Water	$1\frac{1}{2}$ cups
Oyster suace	2–3 tablespoons
Wine	1 tablespoon
Sugar	1 tablespoon
Sesame oil	$\frac{1}{4}$ teaspoon
Cornstarch, use later—blend with 2 tablespoons water	1 tablespoon
Chicken cube, chopped or	1 piece
Monosodium glutamate	1 teaspoon

PROCEDURE

1. Sprinkle salt over bean curd, drain and deep fry in boiling oil until golden brown.
Note: When deep frying bean curd never fry more than 8 pieces at a time, otherwise it will not be crispy.
'Lo Hon' means vegetarian, no meat, something light.
2. Parboil bamboo in boiling water for 1 minute, slice. Soak mushrooms in water for $\frac{1}{2}$ hour, and season with sugar and wine.
Cook bean curd balls with boiling water for 1 minutes, drain.
Light deep-fry olive seeds until brown. Soak snow fungus for $\frac{1}{2}$ hour, drain. Put seasonal vegetable in boiling water, add a little oil and salt, drain.
3. Heat 2–3 tablespoons boiling oil, stir fry all the No. 2 ingredients. Add sauce, and braise over low heat for 5 minutes. Add cornstarch, mix well and pour over fried bean curd. Garnish with vegetables and serve.

Servings: Four to Six
*Can be obtained from your local Chinese delicatessen.

STEAMED BEAN CURD CAKE

四寶豆腐

Ingredients

Lean pork, chopped finely	6 ozs.
*Bean curd	6 pieces
Dried shrimp, soak and chop	1 oz.
Preserved vegetables	2 tablespoons
Spring onion, chopped	2 tablespoon
Parsley, chopped	1 tablespoon
Peanuts, chopped	

Seasoning

Light soy sauce	1 tablespoon
Cornstarch	2 tablespoons
Sesame oil	$\frac{1}{2}$ teaspoon
Pepper	$\frac{1}{4}$ teaspoon
Sugar	$\frac{1}{4}$ teaspoon

(*for bean curd*)

Salt	$\frac{3}{4}$ tablespoon
Oil, small quantity	1 tablespoon

PROCEDURE

1. Marinate pork with the seasoning.
2. Beat up bean curd with a pair of chopsticks, add salt and oil, mix well with lean pork, chopped dried shrimps, preserved vegetables and spring onion. Remove to a deep plate and steam over boiling water for 10 minutes.
3. Sprinkle over chopped parsley and peanuts to serve.

Servings: Three to Four
*Can be obtained at your local Chinese delicatessen.

Mushrooms with Seasonal Vegetables ▶

Overpage Top: Bean Curd with Meat Sauce

Overpage Bottom: Assorted Cold Plate

Overpage Right: Golden Fried Meat Dumpling, Steamed Meat Bun, Steamed Bread

FRIED BEAN CURD WITH MUSHROOMS

雙菇扒豆腐

Ingredients

Fresh or tinned mushrooms	8–10 ozs.
Champignon	1 tin
*Mustard green, or seasonal vegetable	12–16 ozs.
Bean curd, square, fried	8–10 pieces
*Chinese ham, shredded	$\frac{1}{2}$ oz.
Spring onion	4 stalks
Root ginger	2 pieces
Cooking Soda and Salt	
Oil	

Seasoning

Wine	1 tablespoon
Sugar	2 teaspoons

Sauce

Oyster sauce	2 tablespoons
Wine	1 tablespoon
Chicken cube, chopped	1 piece
Water	$\frac{3}{4}$ cup
Sugar	1 teaspoon
Cornstarch	$\frac{1}{2}$ tablespoon

PROCEDURE

1. Blanch fresh mushrooms in water for 1 minute, drain and season with seasoning. Open and use 1 tin or $\frac{1}{2}$ tin champignons and also season with seasoning.
2. Heat 4–5 cups boiling water, add 1 tablespoon oil, 1 pinch of cooking soda, $\frac{1}{2}$ tablespoon salt and cook vegetable for 3 minutes. Drain and arrange around plate.
3. Season bean curd with $\frac{3}{4}$ tablespoon salt, drain and deep fry in 5–6 cups boiling oil until golden brown. Remove to centre of the plate.
4. Heat 2 tablespoon oil in work or skillet, brown spring onions and ginger. Stir fry mushrooms for 2–3 minutes, add sauce and pour over bean curd.

Servings: Six to Eight
*See glossary.

BRAISED BEAN CURD WITH VEGETABLES (Peking)

紅燒豆腐

Ingredients

*Bean curd, Tau Fu	4 squares
Pork loin	3 ozs.
Mushroom, soak and remove stem	5 pieces
Spring onions, chopped	4 stalks
Bamboo shoots, slice and cook	2 ozs.
Carrots, slice and cook	1 oz.
*Mustard green or snow peas, chopped	$\frac{1}{2}$ oz.
Root ginger, shredded	2 pieces
Oil for cooking	

Seasoning

Light soy sauce	1 teaspoon
Sesame oil	$\frac{1}{2}$ teaspoon
Cornstarch	1 teaspoon

Sauce

Water	$\frac{3}{4}$ cup
Salt	$\frac{1}{2}$ teaspoon
Monosodium glutamate	$\frac{1}{2}$ teaspoon
Sugar	$\frac{1}{2}$ teaspoon
Sesame oil	$\frac{1}{2}$ teaspoon
Pepper	$\frac{1}{4}$ teaspoon
Dark soy sauce	1 tablespoon
Cornstarch } use later	$\frac{1}{2}$ tablespoon
Water } use later	$\frac{1}{2}$ tablespoon

PROCEDURE

1. Cut bean curd into $\frac{1}{2}$" pieces. Slice pork loin and marinate in seasoning.
2. Heat 3 tablespoons oil, fry bean curd until light brown then remove to a plate.
3. Heat pan, adding 3 tablespoons oil, stir fry pork slices and mushrooms for 2 minutes. Add spring onions and vegetable and braise with sauce for 3 minutes over medium heat.
4. Thicken above with cornstarch blend with water and serve.

Servings: Four
*See glossary.

◀ Chinese Chicken Noodle Soup

Fried Rice

STEWED EGG PLANT WITH CHILLI SAUCE

辣汁茄子

Ingredients

Chicken fillet, cut into shredded pieces	10 ozs.
Egg plant	12 ozs.
Spring onion, sections	2 stalks
Root ginger, shredded	2 pieces
Soy bean paste	2 tablespoons

Seasoning

Light soy sauce	2 tablesppons
Cornstarch	1½ tablespoons
Sesame oil	1 tablespoon
Sugar	½ teaspoon
Salt	½ teaspoon
Pepper	½ teaspoon
Water	1 tablespoon
Oil	1 tablespoon

Sauce

Water	1½ cups
Shanghai chilli	1 teaspoon
Sesame oil	1 teaspoon
Sugar	1 tablespoon
Salt	½ teaspoon
Cornstarch, use later	1 tablespoon
Chicken cube or	1
Monosodium glutamate	1 teaspoon

PROCEDURE

1. Cut egg plant into 2″ × 1½″ pieces and dry with towel. Fry with 3 tablespoons oil, 1 teaspoon chopped garlic, 1 teaspoon root ginger and 1 tablespoon bean paste. Add sauce and cook for 5 minutes. Remove to a plate. Drain and save the sauce.

2. Heat 2 tablespoon oil, brown spring onion and fry seasoned chicken pieces for 2–3 minutes. To serve, pour the above sauce over egg plant.

Servings: Four to Six.

Soups

湯類

Soup is nutritious and economical and traditionally is

the opening dish at any Chinese meal.

Chinese soups are clear with tasty morsels of meat

and vegetables floating in the broth.

The three soup stock recipes included in this

section are used repeatedly in Chinese cooking and can be the

basic ingredients of more sophisticated soups.

As an alternative to soup at the beginning of the meal

I have included three recipes for assorted cold plates.

These can provide a tasty entree to the meal or

a light snack when friends drop in.

SOUP STOCKS
各種上湯

The following soup stocks are repeatedly used in Chinese cooking:

(1) (High broth) Whole chicken stock
Ingredients

One chicken	3 lbs.
Lean pork	1 lb.
Ham	$\frac{1}{2}$ lb.
Leek, halved and browned	1
Root ginger	5 slices
Water	30 cups

(2) Chicken bone stock
Ingredients

Bone of one whole chicken	
Lean pork (chopped)	4 ozs.
Bone of ham	
Leek, halved and browned	1
Root ginger	4 slices
Water	8 cups

(3) Simple broth

Water	10 cups
Monosodium glutamate or	1 tablespoon
Chicken cube, crushed	1

PROCEDURE (1)
Place chicken, leek and root ginger in water, cover and bring to boil. Lower the heat and boil gently until half the stock has boiled away (about 1–2 hours). Skim the foam from the surface of the water continually. Strain.

PROCEDURE (2)
Wash bones thoroughly. Place bones, pork, ham, leek, and root ginger in the water and heat to boiling. Lower heat and simmer 1 hour. Continually remove foam from surface of the stock. Strain.

PROCEDURE (3)
Cook as for previous soups.

GOLD & SILVER SOUP
金銀瘦肉湯

Ingredients

Lean pork or pork chops	12–16 ozs.
Green turnips, skinned and cut into large pieces	8 ozs.
Carrots, skin and cut in large pieces	8 ozs.
Dried tangerine peel, wash and clean	1 piece
Octopus, optional	4–5 ozs.
Pork chop can be added if desired	8 ozs.
Water	20 cups

Dip
Light soy sauce
Pepper
Sesame oil

PROCEDURE
1. Put lean pork or pork chops in 4 cups boiling water. Parboil for 3 minutes and drain.
2. Wash octopus and soak in water for 20 mintues.
3. Heat 18 cups boiling water in a pot and add lean pork or pork chops, tangerine peel, carrots and green turnips. Bring to boil for 1 hour (high heat), then lower to medium heat.
4. Add octopus to cook for another hour. Season with salt to taste.
5. Mix dip ingredients and serve with soup.

Servings: Six to Seven

BEANCURD & MIXED MEAT SOUP
肉蓉豆腐湯

Ingredients

*Bean curd, cut into cubes	6 pieces
Bamboo shoots, cut into cubes	2 ozs.
Lean pork, cut into cubes	6 ozs.
Shrimp, shelled	4 ozs.
Green pea	2 ozs.
Root ginger, shredded	$\frac{1}{2}$ oz.
Spring onion, shredded	2 stalks
Chicken broth	1 tin

Seasoning
(for pork)

Light soy sauce	1 teaspoon
Pinch of pepper	
Sesame oil, few drops	

(for shrimp)
same as above

PROCEDURE
1. Cut bean curd into cubes.
2. Heat 1 cup chicken broth together with 3 cups water, bring to boil.
3. Cook bean curd together with broth. Mix together with the above ingredients and add a mixture of 3 tablespoons cornstarch and 3 tablespoons water.
4. Add sesame oil and garnish with parsley.

Servings: Six
*See glossary.

ROAST DUCK WITH BAMBOO SHOOT SOUP
火鴨三絲羹

Ingredients

Roast duck shredded	4–6 ozs.
Pork fillet, shredded	3 ozs.
Bamboo shoot, shredded	4 ozs.
Chives, or spring onion, chopped	2 ozs.
Root ginger and spring onion, shredded	1 tablespoon
Chicken broth, add water to make one pot or 1 pot high broth	1 tin

Seasoning

Light soy sauce	1 tablespoon
Cornstarch	$\frac{1}{2}$ tablespoon
Sesame oil	$\frac{1}{4}$ teaspoon
Pepper	$\frac{1}{5}$ teaspoon
Sugar	$\frac{1}{5}$ teaspoon

Oil	1 tablespoon

Sauce

Cornstarch	2 tablespoons
Water	$\frac{1}{4}$ cup
Sesame oil	$\frac{1}{2}$ teaspoon
Light soy sauce	1 tablespoon

PROCEDURE
1. Season shredded pork with the seasoning and let stand for 5 minutes.
2. Open a tin of chicken broth or add high broth (see page 58) add enough water to make a pot. Bring to boil.
3. Add the shredded ingredients, bring to boil, add chives, cornstarch and sauce, and serve.

Variation: Shredded pork, chicken or beef can be substituted.

Servings: Six

STEAMED PIGEON & MUSHROOM SOUP
冬菇雙鴨湯

Ingredients

Pigeon	2
Mushroom, soak and remove stems	2 ozs.
Chicken broth, add water or stock, 1 pot	1 tin
Root ginger	2 pieces
Rock sugar	1 piece
Spring onion	2 stalks

Seasoning
(for pigeon)

Root ginger	2 pieces
Spring onion	1 stalk
Wine	1 teaspoon
Salt	$\frac{1}{2}$ teaspoon

(for mushroom)

Wine	1 tablespoon
Sugar	1 teaspoon

PROCEDURE
1. Heat 5 cups boiling water and parboil pigeons for 5 minutes together with ginger, spring onions and 1 tablespoon wine. Drain, let dry then season and place pigeons in a deep pot.
2. Marinate mushrooms in the seasoning and place in a deep pot.
3. Add chicken broth (or stock) in pot with 1 piece ginger and 1 small lump sugar. Cover, seal with mulberry paper, and steam over boiling water for 3 hours.
4. Before serving, season to taste with salt.

Servings: Five to Six

STEAMED CHICKEN SOUP WITH MUSHROOMS
冬菇燉雞湯

Ingredients

1 Chicken or 4 drum sticks	2 lbs.
Mushroom	3 ozs.
Root ginger	1 piece
Chicken broth	1 tin

Seasoning

Wine	2 tablespoons
Sugar	1 tablespoon
Root ginger	1 piece

PROCEDURE
1. Heat 5 cups boiling water and parboil chicken for 1 minute. Drain.
2. Soak mushrooms for $\frac{1}{2}$ hour, remove stems and season with the seasoning for 5 minutes.
3. In a deep pot add chicken broth and water (5 cups) to the brim. Then add mushrooms and chicken on top and steam over boiling water for 3 hours.
4. Garnish with parsley and ham to serve.

Servings: Four to Five

ASSORTED MEAT WITH MUSHROOM SOUP

冬菇雜會湯

Ingredients

Mushrooms, soak and remove stem	12 pieces
Liver, sliced	4 ozs.
Lean pork, sliced	4 ozs.
Bamboo shoots	2 ozs.
Carrot, sliced	1 oz.
Vegetable, cut into sections and cooked	2 ozs.
Chicken broth, or water and chicken cube	1 tin

Seasoning

(*for mushroom*)

Wine	1 teaspoon
Sugar	$\frac{1}{4}$ teaspoon

(*for pork*)

Salt	$\frac{1}{2}$ teaspoon
Cornstarch	$\frac{1}{2}$ teaspoon
Sesame oil	$\frac{1}{4}$ teaspoon

(*for liver*)

Sesame oil	$\frac{1}{4}$ teaspoon
Pepper	$\frac{1}{4}$ teaspoon
Wine	$\frac{1}{4}$ teaspoon
Ginger juice	$\frac{1}{2}$ teaspoon

PROCEDURE

1. Slice pork fillet and season with seasoning. Let stand for 5 minutes. Soak mushrooms in warm water for $\frac{1}{2}$ hour, remove stem, season with wine and sugar. Cut liver in thin slices and season with above for 5 minutes.

2. Heat 3 cups boiling water, add 2 tablespoons wine and cook pork slices for 1 minute. Drain, then cook liver for 1 minute. Drain and remove to a plate.

3. Add chicken broth and water to make one pot of soup, bring to boil and cook bamboo shoots and carrots for 2 minutes. Add pork, liver and vegetable. Add 1 tablespoon salt and $\frac{1}{4}$ teaspoon sesame oil and serve.

Servings: Four to Six

SLICED BEEF WITH WATERCRESS SOUP

西洋菜牛肉湯

Ingredients

Beef steak, rump or fillet	4 ozs.
Watercress	6 ozs.
Chicken broth, or stock	2 cups
Water	3 cups
Salt and pepper to taste	

Seasoning

Corn flour	2 teaspoons
Water	$\frac{1}{2}$ teaspoon
Sesame oil	a few drops

PROCEDURE

1. Cut beef with sharp knife into $1'' \times \frac{1}{2}''$ paper thin slices. Marinate in seasoning for 10 minutes.

2. Clean watercress thoroughly with water, washing 2–3 times.

3. Heat broth and bring to boil. Add watercress and simmer in the broth for 4–5 minutes. Add beef, salt and pepper to taste and serve after 2 minutes.

Servings: Four

BEAN SPROUT WITH LEAN PORK SOUP (Szechuan)

芽菜肉片湯

Ingredients

Bean sprouts	6 ozs.
Lean pork, sliced	4 ozs.
Root ginger, shredded	1 piece
Water	6 cups
Cornstarch	$\frac{1}{4}$ teaspoon

Seasoning

Salt	1 tablespoon
Monosodium glutamate	1 teaspoon

PROCEDURE

1. Cut and slice lean pork. Mix well with $\frac{1}{4}$ teaspoon cornstarch and 1 teaspoon water.

2. Heat 6 cups boiling water, add 1 piece ginger, pork slices and simmer for 10 minutes. Then add bean sprouts and cook for another 10 minutes.

3. Put in salt and monosodium glutamate, place in a serving bowl and serve.

Servings: Five

ASSORTED COLD PLATE

三拼冷盆

(1) Sea Jelly
(2) Chicken in wine ⎫ servings six to eight
(3) Pig's tongue ⎭

(1) *SEA JELLY*
Ingredients
*Sea jelly, washed, soaked and
    seasoned   8 ozs.

Seasoning
Light soy sauce	1 tablespoon
Monosodium glutamate	1 teaspoon
Sesame oil	1 teaspoon
Cooked oil	1 tablespoon

PROCEDURE
1. Wash sea jelly a few times with water, and soak in cold water over-night.
2. Rinse with cooled, boiled water. Dry with a towel.
3. Shred into pieces, and season as above and serve.

*Available from Chinese delicatessen

(2) *CHICKEN IN WINE*
Ingredients
1 chicken	2½ lbs.
Root ginger	1 piece
Spring onion	1 stalk
*Yellow wine	¾ bottle

Seasoning
Salt	1 tablespoon
Wine	1 tablespoon
Root ginger	1 piece
Spring onion	1 stalk

PROCEDURE
1. Clean chicken and dry with a towel. Season inside and outside of chicken with salt. Put wine, ginger and spring onion inside the chicken. Let stand for 10 minutes.
2. Steam over boiling water for 25 minutes.
3. Cut chicken into 4–6 large pieces, and soak in ½ bottle yellow wine for 4 hours.
4. Cut into bite-size pieces and serve.

*Chinese wine or sherry.

(3) *PIG'S TONGUE:*
Ingredients
Pig's tongue	4–6 pieces

Spicy sauce
Light soy sauce	1 cup
Dark soy sauce	½ cup
Water	2 cups
Root ginger	1 piece
Spring onion	2 stalks
Sugar	½ cup
Wine	1 tablespoon
Aniseed	4 cloves

PROCEDURE
1. Clean pig's tongue and put in boiling water for 5 minutes. Scrap it clean with a knife, then wash and dry.
2. Bring spicy sauce to boil. Cook pig's tongue for an hour. Drain and brush with sesame oil. Slice into thin pieces and serve.

ASSORTED MEAT WITH TAU FU SOUP

八珍豆腐湯

Ingredients

*Bean curd, cut into cubes	8 pieces
Lean pork, cut into cubes and season with 1 teaspoon salt	10 ozs.
Bamboo shoot	4 ozs.
Mushroom, cubes	4 ozs.
Shrimp, shelled and seasoned with pepper and sesame oil	6 ozs.
Green peas	4 ozs.
Chives, chopped	9 ozs.
Chicken broth and water	6 cups
Oil for cooking	

Seasoning

Light soy sauce	1 tablespoon
Pepper	$\frac{1}{4}$ teaspoon
Cornstarch	$\frac{1}{2}$ tablespoon
Sesame oil	$\frac{1}{4}$ teaspoon

Sauce

Water	$\frac{1}{4}$ cup
Light soy sauce	1 teaspoon
Cornstarch	3–4 tablespoons
Monosodium glutamate	1 teaspoon
Salt to taste	

PROCEDURE

1. Cook bean curd with water and chicken broth. Bring to boil.
2. Season pork cubes and shrimps with the seasoning.
3. Quick wash in 2 cups of boiling water for 1 minute, drain and cook all the above ingredients together in chicken broth.
4. Mix sauce ingredients with enough salt to taste and serve.

Servings: Six to Seven
*See glossary.

HOT & SOUR SOUP

酸辣湯

Ingredients

Chicken liver	3 ozs.
*Bean curd, cut into long strips	2 cakes
Shredded pork, season with light soy sauce, cornstarch and sesame oil	3 ozs.
Bamboo shoot, shredded	3 ozs.
Dried shrimp, soaked	2 tablespoons
Egg	2
*Wood ear, soaked and shredded	$\frac{1}{2}$ oz.
Chicken broth or stock, add water to make 1 big bowl	1 tin
Spring onion or parsley, chopped	2 stalks

Seasoning for soup

Light soy sauce	1 tablespoon
Salt	1 teaspoon
Vinegar, add later	2 tablespoons
Pepper	$\frac{1}{2}$ teaspoon
Sugar	$\frac{1}{4}$ teaspoon

Thickening sauce

Cornstarch	3 tablespoons
Sesame oil	1 teaspoon
Dark soy sauce, for colour	

PROCEDURE

1. Heat 2 tablespoons oil, fry shredded bamboo and pork, add chicken stock and bring to boil.
2. Then add bean curd, liver, wood ear and dried shrimp. Add the Seasoning, simmer for 2–3 minutes, then add vinegar and pepper. Stir in cornstarch paste to thicken, pour in beaten eggs and chives and serve.

Servings: Six to Eight
*See glossary.

SLICED PORK & MUSHROOM SOUP

磨菇瘦肉片湯

Ingredients

Lean pork	4 ozs.
Button mushrooms	$\frac{3}{4}$ cup
Seasonal vegetables	2 ozs.
Chicken broth	3 cups
Water	2 cups
Pepper and salt to taste	
Sherry	1 teaspoon

Seasoning

Cornstarch	$\frac{1}{2}$ teaspoon
Light soy sauce	1 teaspoon
Sesame oil	$\frac{1}{4}$ teaspoon
Water and oil	1 tablespoon

PROCEDURE

1. Cut lean pork into $1'' \times \frac{1}{2}''$ pieces and marinate in seasoning. Let stand for 10 minutes.
2. Cut button mushrooms into thin pieces and cut seasonal vegetable into $2''$ sections.
3. Heat broth and when it starts to boil, add pork, vegetable and mushrooms.
4. Let it simmer for 5 minutes. Season to taste with salt, pepper and sherry and serve.

Servings: Two

Rice and Noodles
飯，麵．

Rice, as we all know is the staple diet of the majority of mankind.

For centuries it has provided the essential protein and

other nutrients to the peoples of Asia.

It is indeed impossible to think of

Chinese cooking without rice and the

variety of recipes using it are endless.

The long-grain variety is considered the most

suitable for Chinese cooking.

Noodles are made from a mixture of flour, eggs and water.

Contrary to popular belief they are not fattening

as they do not absorb fluids.

In China over 40 different varieties of noodles are obtainable.

Noodles go particularly well with vegetables.

FRIED GAROUPA RICE WITH ASPARAGUS SAUCE

露筍班球飯

Ingredients

Garoupa or other fish fillet, cubed	12 ozs.
Asparagus, chopped	1 tin
Green peas	4 tablespoons
Carrot, cooked, chopped	2 tablespoons
Spring Onion, chopped	3 ozs.
Rice, cooked	1 lb.

Seasoning

Light soy sauce	1 tablespoon
Salt	1 teaspoon
Sesame oil	1 teaspoon
Cornstarch	1 tablespoon
Sugar	$\frac{1}{4}$ teaspoon
Pepper	$\frac{1}{4}$ teaspoon
Water	$\frac{1}{2}$ tablespoon
Oil	$\frac{1}{2}$ tablespoon

Sauce

Chicken broth or water	1 cup
Sesame oil	1 tablespoon
Cornstarch	1 tablespoon
Salt	1 teaspoon
Sugar	1 pinch
Milk	$\frac{1}{3}$ cup

PROCEDURE

1. Marinate fish in seasoning and stand for 10 minutes.

2. Heat 3 tablespoons oil, brown ginger, onions and fry fish cubes. Add green peas, asparagus and carrots. Mix well with sauce, bring to boil and pour over rice to serve.

Servings: Five to Six

ASSORTED NOODLES IN POT

楊州窩麵

Ingredients

*Cake noodles	6 ozs.
Chives or seasonal vegetable, cooked in water for 2 minutes	1 oz.
Ham, shredded	1 oz.
Liver, cooked and sliced	1 oz.
Lean pork, cooked and sliced	2 ozs.
Roast pork, optional	1 oz.
Shrimp, cooked	2 ozs.
Broth	1 tin
Water	5 cups
Mushroom	6 pieces
Monosodium glutamate	2 teaspoons
Oil for cooking	
Soy sauce	1 tablespoon
Sesame oil	$\frac{1}{4}$ teaspoon
Pepper and salt to taste	

PROCEDURE

1. Put noodles in boiling water and loosen with chopsticks.

2. Heat 4 cups boiling water, parboil liver, lean pork, roast pork, shrimps and mushrooms for 1–2 minutes. Drain, then put aside.

3. Bring broth and 5 cups of water to boil then add noodles.

4. Then put all the assorted meat and vegetables on top of noodles, sprinkle soy sauce, pepper and sesame oil, and serve. Season to taste with salt.

Servings: Four
*See glossary.

CHINESE CHICKEN NOODLE SOUP

雞絲湯麵

Ingredients

*Cake noodles	4–5 ozs.
Chicken broth	3 cups
Chicken, cooked and shredded	3–4 tablespoons
Ham, shredded	1 oz.
Light soy sauce	1 teaspoon
Sesame oil	$\frac{1}{4}$ teaspoon
Pepper and salt to taste	

PROCEDURE

1. Heat 4 cups boiling water, add noodles and loosen them with a pair of chopsticks. Drain and place in bowl.

2. Heat broth, bring to boil, then add noodles and place shredded chicken and ham on top.

3. Season to taste with light soy sauce, sesame oil, pepper and salt to taste.

Servings: Two
*Buy from Chinese delicatessen.

BEEF FU YUNG WITH NOODLES

滑蛋牛肉麵

Ingredients

Beef fillet, sliced thinly	10 ozs.
*Cake noodles	6–8 ozs.
Eggs	6
Root ginger	2 pieces
Spring onion, or onion	2 stalks
Garlic	1 piece
Oil for cooking	

Seasoning

Water	season for	1 tablespoon
Bicarbonate of soda	1 hour.	$\frac{1}{2}$ teaspoon
Cornstarch		1 tablespoon
Sesame oil		$\frac{1}{4}$ teaspoon
Pepper		$\frac{1}{4}$ teaspoon
Water		1 tablespoon
Oil		1 tablespoon
Sugar		$\frac{1}{2}$ teaspoon

PROCEDURE

1. Marinate beef slices in seasoning and allow to stand for 10 minutes.
2. Heat 6 cups boiling water, loosen cake noodles and cook for 1 minute. Drain and run cold water over noodles. Drain again and add 2 tablespoons cooked oil. Mix well.
3. Heat 3 tablespoon oil, brown garlic and fry noodles on both sides until light brown. Sprinkle 1 teaspoon salt on each side of noodles, remove when brown to a serving plate.
4. Beat eggs together with 1 teaspoon salt.
5. Heat a lot of oil and quick deep fry beef pieces for 2 minutes. Drain and remove to a plate.
6. Heat 2 tablespoons oil, brown ginger and spring onions. Fry beef and pour in beaten eggs and mix well together. Pour over noodles and serve.

Servings: Six to Seven
*Obtainable at Chinese delicatessen.

FRIED RICE (Chow Fan)

揚州炒飯

Ingredients

Cold cooked rice	1 lb.
Eggs	4
Roast pork or ham, cut into small cubes	4 ozs.
Shrimp, steam and shelled	10 ozs.
Onions, cut into small pieces	4 ozs.
Green peas	4 ozs.
Oil	

Sauce

Monosodium glutamate	1 teaspoon
Light soy sauce	2 tablespoons

PROCEDURE

1. Put beaten eggs in pan, add 2 tablespoons oil and stir fry for 1 minute. Chop into small pieces.
2. Heat 2 tablespoons oil, stir fry chopped onions and rice. Mix with eggs.
3. Add ham and shrimps and sprinkle with 1 tablespoon light soy sauce. Mix well and serve.

Servings: Six to Eight

ASSORTED MEAT WITH CONGEE

三及第粥

Ingredients

Rice	1 cup
Water	14 cups
Oil	$\frac{1}{2}$ teaspoon
Salt	$\frac{1}{2}$ teaspoon
Liver, sliced	6 ozs.
Lean pork, chopped finely	8 ozs.
Fish fillet, cut up	6 ozs.
Fried rice noodle	1 cake
Root ginger, shredded	2 pieces
Spring onion, chredded	4 stalks

Seasoning

(for liver, lean pork and fish fillet separately)

Light soy sauce	1 teaspoon
Cornstarch	1 teaspoon
Sesame oil	$\frac{1}{2}$ teaspoon
Salt	$\frac{1}{2}$ teaspoon
Water and oil	1 teaspoon
Pepper	$\frac{1}{4}$ teaspoon

Sauce

Light soy sauce	$\frac{1}{2}$ tablespoon
Sesame, for dips	$\frac{1}{4}$ teaspoon
Pepper	$\frac{1}{4}$ teaspoon

PROCEDURE

1. Marinate pork with seasoning and make meat balls. Marinate liver and fish with seasoning for 10 minutes.
2. Rinse rice until water runs clear, mix well with oil and salt. Add 14 cups of water and bring to the boil, (turn heat to medium), and keep cooking for $\frac{3}{4}$ hour, until it thickens to congee. If too thick add water.
3. Add liver pieces, meat balls in congee, and cook for 3 minutes. Add fish slices, mixed with ginger and spring onions. Add salt to taste and serve.

Variation: Fried dumplings and fried rice noodles go well with congee.

FRIED SINGAPORE RICE NOODLES
星州炒米粉

Ingredients

Rice noodles	8 ozs.
Bean sprouts	4 ozs.
Chives, cut into sections	2 ozs.
Roast pork or ham, shredded	6 ozs.
Pickled ginger, shredded	2 ozs.
Spring onion, shredded	5 stalks
Root ginger	1 piece
Curry powder	1 teaspoon
Eggs, beaten	3
Oil for cooking	
Salt	1 teaspoon
Broth	1 tablespoon
Sesame oil	$\frac{1}{4}$ teaspoon
Soy sauce	2 tablespoons

PROCEDURE

1. Soak rice noodles in warm water for 10 minutes and then drain.
2. Heat 2 tablespoon oil in frying pan or wok. Fry beaten egg and make into a pan cake. Cut into narrow pieces. Remove to a plate and set aside.
3. Heat pan or wok, add 1 tablespoon oil. Empty oil and stir fry bean sprouts for 2 minutes, together with one piece of ginger and $\frac{1}{2}$ teaspoon salt.
4. Heat 2 tablespoons oil in frying pan or wok. When hot, stir fry pork pieces, pickled ginger and chives for 1–2 minutes. Remove to a plate.
5. Heat 2 tablespoons oil in a pan or wok, brown garlic, and stir fry rice noodles for about 2–3 minutes. Sprinkle with 1 teaspoon salt and 1 tablespoon broth. Mix well with all the above ingredients together with sesame oil and soy sauce and serve. Garnish with shredded eggs and parsley.

Servings: Four

Tips: Remember to use a pair of chopsticks when stir frying rice noodles, so that the noodles will not break into short sections.

SEA FOOD RICE SUPREME
雙色海鮮飯

Ingredients

Rice, cold	14–16 ozs.
Shrimp, shelled	14–16 ozs.
Garoupa, cut into cubes	14–16 ozs.
Green peas	4 ozs.
Onion, chopped finely	3 ozs.
Onion, shredded	4 ozs.
Green pepper, shredded	2–4 ozs.
Eggs, beaten	3–4

Seasoning

(for garoupa)

Salt	1 teaspoon
Cornstarch	1 tablespoon
Sesame oil	$\frac{1}{4}$ teaspoon
Pepper	$\frac{1}{4}$ teaspoon
Oil	$\frac{1}{2}$ tablespoon
Water	$\frac{1}{2}$ tablespoon

(for shrimp)

Salt	1 teaspoon
Sesame oil	$\frac{1}{2}$ teaspoon
Pepper	$\frac{1}{4}$ teaspoon
Cornstarch	$\frac{3}{4}$ teaspoon

Sauce

(White sauce for garoupa)

Water or chicken broth	$\frac{3}{4}$ cup
Cornstarch	1 tablespoon
Sesame oil	$\frac{1}{2}$ teaspoon
Monosodium glutamate	1 teaspoon
Evaporated milk	$\frac{1}{3}$ tin (small)

(Tomato sauce for shrimp)

Water	$\frac{3}{4}$ cup
Tomato sauce	3 tablespoons
Tomato paste	$\frac{1}{2}$ cup
Sugar	$\frac{3}{4}$ tablespoon
Light soy sauce	1 teaspoon
Cornstarch	1 tablespoon
Chicken cube	1
Pinch of salt	

PROCEDURE

1. Heat 2 tablespoons oil in wok and fry beaten eggs for 1 minute then chop into small pieces.
2. Heat 2 tablespoons oil, stir fry onions and mix well with rice and eggs. Add $\frac{3}{4}$ tablespoon salt and remove to a plate.
3. Heat 2–3 tablespoons oil in wok, fry shredded onions and fish cubes. Add white sauce and green peas. Bring to boil and remove to a bowl.
4. Heat 2 tablespoons oil, fry onions, shrimps and tomato sauce. Bring to boil and remove to a bowl.
5. Put white sauce on one side of fried rice and tomato sauce on the other side. Arrange fried shredded pepper in a cross shape in the middle and garnish with parsley.

Servings: Six to Eight

DIM SUM-Pastries, Bread and Desserts
點心，甜品．

I have devoted this last section to Dim Sum.

Included are recipes which can be used to

finish the meal or provide tasty snacks for

the usual Dim Sum hour.

I have found most of these recipes very popular

and recommend that they all be tried.

SWEET POTATOES WITH HONEY

蜜餞薯條

Ingredients

Sweet potatoes	1½ lbs.
Water	3 cups

Honey syrup

Honey or malt	3 talbespoons
Sugar	6 tablespoons
Vinegar	½ tablespoon
Water	2 cups

PROCEDURE

1. Remove skin from potatoes, then cut into long sticks about ½″ thick and 4″ long. Cook in boiling water for 10 minutes then drain.
2. Combine syrup ingredients and bring to the boil.
3. Cook potato sticks for 40 minutes over low heat, until the potatoes are tender.

To Serve

Arrange potatoes on a serving plate and pour over sauce.

Servings: Five

SAGO PUDDING

西米布甸

Ingredients

Sago	6 ozs.
Water	5 cups
Custard powder	3 tablespoons
Condensed milk	1½ tablespoons
Butter	2½ ozs.
Egg	3
*Lotus seed paste	4 ozs.
Vanilla essence	2 drops
Sugar	5 tablespoons

PROCEDURE

1. Soak sago in water for 1 hour.
2. Heat oven to 350°F.
3. Beat eggs well and mix custard powder with water.
4. Put butter in boiling water, add sago, sugar and condensed milk.
5. Add custard powder and eggs into above mixture and cook for 1 minute.
6. Put 1 bowl of the above mixture at the bottom of a deep plate, add lotus seed paste and cover the top with the rest of the mixture. Put in oven for 5 minutes and serve.

Servings: Four

*Can be obtained at local chinese store.

VEGETABLE & PORK BUN

菜肉飽

Ingredients

Flour	5 cups
Sugar	3 tablespoons
Water	2 cups
Baking powder	2 teaspoons
Yeast	2 teaspoons

Stuffing

Lean pork, chopped fine	10 ozs.
Chinese cabbage, cooked and chopped	1 lb.

Seasoning

Light soy sauce	1 tablespoon
Monosodium glutamate	½ teaspoon
Sugar	¼ teaspoon
Pepper	¼ teaspoon

Chives or spring onion, chopped 2 ozs.

PROCEDURE

1. Mix pork well with cooked and chopped vegetable. Add spring onions and the seasoning. Use as stuffing.
2. **Basic Yeast Dough**—Dissolve yeast in water. Pour flour on the table or a board, making a hole in the centre. Add water and yeast, mix well then add sugar and baking powder, knead well and let rise for 10 minutes.
3. Roll the risen dough into a long roll and divide into 20 pieces. Roll each piece of dough into a ball and flatten with palm of hand into a 4″ circle.
4. Put one portion of filling in the middle of the dough circle, and gather the edges in with the thumb and forefinger.
5. Steam over boiling water for 15 minutes.

Servings: Twenty

STEAMED ROAST PORK BUN
叉燒飽

Ingredients

Flour	$2\frac{1}{2}$ cups
Sugar	$1\frac{1}{2}$ tablespoons
Water	1 cup
Baking powder	1 teaspoon
Dry yeast	1 teaspoon
Oil for cooking	

To make dough circle for roast
    pork bun please see basic
yeast dough on page (64)

Stuffing

Roast pork	8–10 ozs.
Water	1 cup
Sesame oil	1 teaspoon
Oyster sauce	$1\frac{1}{2}$ tablespoons
Light soy sauce	1 tablespoon
Hoi Sin sauce	1 tablespoon
Monosodium glutamate	1 teaspoon
Sugar	3 tablespoons
Cornstarch, blend with water, add later	2 tablespoons
Root ginger	1 piece
Spring onions	2 stalks

PROCEDURE

1. Cut roast pork into small cubes $\frac{1}{2}'' \times \frac{1}{2}''$.
2. Heat oil, brown spring onions and ginger and add all the stuffing ingredients. Bring to boil. Mix with the roast pork let cool and set.
3. After making dough circle place one portion of filling in the middle, pleat edges of circle and press firmly, wrap up, press the entire circle and close.
4. Place ready-made buns on square of paper and let rise for 16 minutes. Arrange buns in bamboo rack steamer, and steam for 10 minutes.

Variations
The same dough can be made into chicken bun, pork bun, or sausage bun.
Sweet lotus paste and red dates can be used as filling.

Servings: Five to Six

TARO CAKES
酥炸芋角

Ingredients
(for wrappings or skin)

Peeled Taro Root	1 lb.
Lard	$4\frac{1}{2}$ tablespoons
Cornstarch	3 tablespoons
Salt	$\frac{1}{2}$ teaspoon
Sugar	$\frac{3}{4}$ tablespoon
Oil for deep frying	

(for the stuffing)

Lean pork	4 ozs.
Shrimps, shelled	2 ozs.
Mushrooms	4 pieces
Egg yolk	1
Garlic	1 teaspoon

Seasoning
(for lean pork)

Soy sauce	$\frac{1}{2}$ tablespoon
Cornstarch	1 teaspoon

(for shrimps)

Sugar	$\frac{1}{4}$ tablespoon
Salt	$\frac{1}{2}$ teaspoon
Sesame oil	$\frac{1}{4}$ teaspoon
Pepper	$\frac{1}{5}$ teaspoon
Water	$\frac{1}{4}$ cup

PROCEDURE

1. Cut lean pork into little cubes and season with cornstarch and light soy sauce.
2. Shell shrimps and cut into small cubes.
3. Soak mushrooms and cut into small cubes.
4. Heat 2 tablespoons oil, brown garlic and stir fry lean pork, shrimps and mushrooms for 2 minutes. Mix well with egg yolk and seasoning. To be used as filling.
5. Steam taro until soft and mash. Add $2\frac{1}{2}$ ozs. *Tang flour (豆粉), lard, sugar, and salt. Knead well and roll into a long sausage then cut into pieces and press into a round circle (3″).
6. Add one portion filling and fold in half to make a semi-circle shape. Then pinch edges to seal.
7. Heat oil and deep fry taro cakes until light golden brown. Drain and serve.

Servings: Four to Five
*See glossary.

ALMOND TEA
杏仁茶

Ingredients
Almond	6 ozs.
Rice	3 ozs.
Fresh milk	1 cup
Sugar	8 ozs.
Water	10 cups

PROCEDURE
1. Soak almonds in hot water and remove skin.
2. Put almonds, rice and a little water into a mixer and grind until fine.
3. Put almond paste in strainer and add cold water.
4. Put the mixture in a pot, add sugar and bring to the boil. Serve together with pineapple or orange.

STEAMED MEAT BUN
菜肉飽

Ingredients
Flour	10 ozs.
Boiling water	1 cup
Cold water	1 oz.

Filling
Lean pork, dried	8 ozs.
Fat pork, cubed	1 oz.
Mushroom, chopped	4 pieces
Chives or spring onion, chopped	2 ozs.

Seasoning
Dark soy sauce	1 teaspoon
Salt	$\frac{1}{2}$ teaspoon
Sugar	1 teaspoon
Sesame oil	$\frac{1}{4}$ teaspoon
Pepper	$\frac{1}{4}$ teaspoon
Wine	$\frac{1}{2}$ teaspoon
Cornstarch	1 teaspoon
Water	1 tablespoon

PROCEDURE
1. In a mixing bowl add flour boiling and cold water. Stir and mix well.
2. Wet hands with cold water, place flour mixture on the table, and knead into a soft dough.
3. Put the filling ingredients into a deep bowl, add cornstarch and seasoning, pound and mix well.
4. Knead soft dough into a long roll, divide into 24 pieces and roll into thin round sheets.
5. Put the round dough on left hand. Add one portion of filling. Pinch edges together to form a bun.
6. Put a few pieces of vegetable leaves in a steamer and put buns on top. Steam for 5 minutes and serve

Servings: Five to Six

SHRIMP DUMPLING
鮮蝦餃

Ingredients
Shrimp	1 lb.
Fat pork, cubed	3 ozs.
Bamboo, shredded	3 ozs.
*Tang flour (豆粉)	8 ozs.
Water	5 ozs.
Cornstarch	1 teaspoon

Seasoning
Salt	1 teaspoon
Sugar	2 tablespoons
Monosodium Glutamate	1 teaspoon
Pepper	$\frac{1}{4}$ teaspoon
Lard	1 tablespoon

PROCEDURE
1. Shell shrimps, cut into little pieces and rub dry with a towel. Add seasoning, pork, bamboo and lard. Mix well and put into the refrigerator for 1 hour.
2. **Dumpling Preparation**—Put Tang flour (豆粉) in a deep bowl, add water, mix well and knead into a dough. Add lard, knead again, and roll into a long sausage. Cut into 40 pieces.
3. Using cleaver blade, flatten dough into paper-thin circles about 2 inches diameter. Gather edges with the thumb and fore-fingers and make into shrimp dumplings.
4. Steam over boiling water for 5 minutes and serve.

Servings: Five
*See glossary.

WALNUT CAKE
合桃酥

Ingredients

Flour	1 lb.
Sugar	8 ozs.
Lard	6 ozs.
Egg Yolk	1
Bicarbonate of soda	1 teaspoon
Walnuts	

PROCEDURE

1. Mix lard and sugar, then add egg and bicarbon- ate of soda. Mix well, then add flour. Rub well together, flatten with palm of hand and cut into 3–4 pieces, putting one on top of the other.
2. Roll the above into a long roll and divide into 24 round pieces, making a hole in the middle. Place a piece of walnut inside the hole. Brush with egg yolk and place over a greased rack.
3. Put walnut cake in the oven for 35 minutes (medium heat). It is ready to serve when a light golden brown.

Servings: Twenty-Four

STEAMED BREAD
花卷

Ingredients

Flour	$2\frac{1}{2}$ cups
Sugar	$1\frac{1}{2}$ tablespoon
Water	1 cup
Dry yeast	1 teaspoon
Baking powder	1 teaspoon

PROCEDURE

1. Put 1 teaspoon yeast in 1 cup water and let dissolve.
2. Put flour on the table or on a board and make a hole in the middle. Add yeast mixture.
3. Knead the above until smooth (5 minutes.)
4. Add sugar and baking powder into the kneaded dough. Knead again and mix well (5 minutes) and roll into a long sausage.
5. Press the dough flat with the palm of the hands and using a rolling pin make it into a shape 12″ × 9″ × $\frac{2}{5}$″ thick.
6. Add 1 tablespoon oil over the surface and sprinkle $\frac{1}{2}$ tablespoon flour then roll the dough and cut into 2″ long pieces.
7. Press the dough in the middle with one chopstick. Roll again and press with one chop stick in the middle.
8. Steam over a rack steamer in boiling water for 15 minutes and serve.

Servings: Five to Six

SPRING ROLL SHEETS
春卷皮做法

Ingredients

Flour	3 cups
Water	$1\frac{1}{2}$ cups
Salt	$\frac{3}{4}$ teaspoon
Oil, for oiling grill	

PROCEDURE

1. In a bowl, add sifted flour, salt and water gradually. Mix well, until dough is smooth. Add $\frac{1}{8}$ cup of water on top of dough to keep it from getting dry. Let stand and rise for $\frac{1}{2}$ hour.
2. Pick up a portion of the dough surrounding the edge of the bowl and drop it into the centre of the bowl. Repeat this process a few times.
3. Place a flat, heavy grill over medium heat, and oil grill with an oil-soaked cloth. Lightly grill dough in a circular motion, to make a 6″ paper thin pancake.
4. Peel spring roll sheet off grill or pan and remove to a serving plate. Repeat until 20 sheets are made. If grill is too hot, take away from the heat. Oil before making each new sheet.

Servings: Twenty sheets

CHINESE PANCAKE WITH DATE PASTE
棗泥窩餅

Ingredients
Flour	4 tablespoons
Egg, beaten	1
Water	7 tablespoons
Date paste or lotus paste	3 ozs.

PROCEDURE
1. Add water in flour and mix well, then add the beaten egg and stir.

2. Heat 2 tablespoons oil, and when hot, empty all the oil, except one tablespoon. Add egg mixture, and lower the heat, until a round piece of thin pancake is made. Remove from heat.

3. Add 1 piece 5″ × 4″ of thin date paste in the centre of pancake, then fold up the 4 sides, and fry until golden brown, together with 2 tablespoons oil. Cut into pieces and serve.

Servings: Two

SHIU MAE
燒賣

Ingredients
Lean pork, diced	10 ozs.
Fat pork, diced	1 oz.
*Chinese mushrooms, soak and cut into cubes	4 pieces
Bamboo shoots, diced, cooked and dried	
*Wanton sheets	30 pieces
Carrots, chopped	$\frac{1}{4}$ cup
Chinese cariander, parsley	$\frac{1}{4}$ cup

Seasoning
Cornstarch	1 tablespoon
Salt	1 teaspoon
Pepper	$\frac{1}{4}$ teaspoon
Sesame oil	$\frac{1}{2}$ teaspoon
Sherry	$\frac{1}{2}$ teaspoon
Sugar	$\frac{1}{2}$ teaspoon
Monosodium glutamate	1 teaspoon
Egg white	1

PROCEDURE
1. Put lean pork, fat pork, mushrooms and bamboo shoots together in a bowl and marinate in seasoning for 10 minutes.

2. Trim wanton sheets to round circles and place 1 portion stuffing in the centre of wanton sheets Gather edges together to make a waist and press down filling with a spoon.

3. Put all Shiu Mae on a round plate and steam over boiling water for 5 minutes (high heat) and then serve.

Servings: Four to Six
*See glossary.

ALMOND JELLY
杏仁豆腐

Ingredients
(for No. 1 mixture)
*Agar Agar	$\frac{1}{2}$oz.
Water	6 cups
Evaporated milk	$\frac{1}{2}$ cup
Almond essence	1 teaspoon
Sugar	1 cup

(for No. 2 mixture)
Sugar	2 cups
Water	6 cups

(for No. 3 mixture)
Mandarin oranges in syrup, or mixed fruit	1 tin

PROCEDURE
1. Pour No. 1 mixture into a pan. Bring to boil until the agar agar is completely dissolved. Then pour into a square pan and let cool. When the mixture has set, cut into bite-size squares.

2. Bring No. 2 mixture to the boil When it is cool, add the almond jelly cubes and the tin of mandarin oranges.

Servings: Eight
*See glossary.

8 TREASURE RICE PUDDING
八寶糯米飯

Ingredients

Glutinous rice	2 cups
Cold water	2 cups
Sugar	5 tablespoons
Red bean paste, or lotus seed paste or red date paste	½ lb.
Lard	
Dried fruits or nuts	2 ozs.
Lotus seed	2 ozs.
Raisins	2 ozs.
Red or green cherries	2 ozs.
Chestnuts, boiled	2 ozs.

Sauce

Water	1½ cup
Sugar	2 teaspoons
Cornstarch	1 teaspoon

PROCEDURE

1. Clean rice 2–3 times, then mix rice with water and steam or boil for 3 minutes. Add sugar and stir well.
2. Grease the inside of a 7″ bowl with lard and place all the dried fruits into the bowl. Arrange in a pattern and then place one portion of rice in bowl over the fruit arrangement, add red bean paste, and then allow the other portion of rice to form another final layer. Steam rice pudding for 20 minutes.
3. Boil sauce mixture, stirring constantly.
4. Using spatula to loosen edges, turn rice pudding out of the bowl onto a large plate. Pour hot sauce over pudding and serve.

Servings: Five to Six

SPRING ROLL
酥炸春卷

Ingredients

Lean pork, cut into fine strips	8 ozs.
Chives, chopped	2 ozs.
Shrimps, steam and shell	8 ozs.
Dried mushroom, soaked and shredded	6 pieces
Bamboo shoots, shredded	2 ozs.
*Spring Roll Sheets	
Flour and water	2 tablespoons
Oil for deep frying	

Seasoning

Salt	1 teaspoon
Pepper	1 teaspoon
Sugar	1 teaspoon
Wine	1 tablespoon
Light soy sauce	1 teaspoon
Monosodium glutamate	1 teaspoon

PROCEDURE

1. Mix pork with salt, pepper, sugar, wine and light soy sauce.
2. Heat 2 tablespoons oil, brown garlic and fry pork mixture. Add shrimps and chives. Remove from heat.
3. Place a small amount of this mixture on pieces of flour wrapping and wrap in rolls, pasted with flour and water mixture. Fry in a deep oil until crispy and serve.

Servings: Twenty approximately
*From your Chinese store, or see recipe Page 67.

STEAMED TURNIP CAKE WITH ASSORTED DRIED MEAT
八寶蘿蔔糕

Ingredients

Turnip, shredded	4–5 lbs.
Rice powder or cornstarch	12 ozs.
Mushroom, soaked, chopped	1 oz.
Dried shrimp, soaked	3 ozs.
*Chinese sausage, chopped	6 ozs.
*Chinese dried pork, chopped	4 ozs.
Parsley	2 ozs.
Lard	2 tablespoons
Sugar	1 teaspoon
Monosodium glutamate	1 teaspoon
Salt	1 tablespoon
Sesame seed	2 ozs.
Pepper	1 teaspoon

PROCEDURE

1. Heat 2 tablespoons oil, fry turnip and cook until soft. Add salt and monosodium glutamate. Drain water away and put into a pot.
2. Add rice powder to turnip water and mix well. Fry mushrooms, dried shrimps, Chinese sausage and dried pork.
3. Add the above ingredients to turnip and mix well. Pour into a deep pan. Steam over boiling water for 1 hour.
4. Sprinkle parsley and fried sesame seed over top.
To serve: Slice into pieces when cold.

Servings: Thirty, depending on size of pieces cut.
*Can be obtained at your Chinese delicatessen.

SNOW FUNGUS WITH LYCHEE

雪耳荔枝羹

Ingredients
*Fungus, soaked	$\frac{1}{2}$ oz.
Lychee	1 can
Pineapple	1 can
Sugar	6–8 ozs.

PROCEDURE

1. Soak snow fungus in hot water for $\frac{1}{2}$ hour.
2. Put sugar into 7 cups of water and bring to boil.
3. Cook fungus for 20 minutes in the sweet water then freeze until cold. Add lychee and pineapple on top and serve. An excellent Chinese dessert for summer.

*See glossary.

GOLDEN FRIED MEAT DUMPLING (Peking)

窩貼

Ingredients
Lean pork	6 ozs.
Chives, chopped	6 ozs.

Seasoning
Salt	$\frac{1}{2}$ teaspoon
Monosodium glutamate	$\frac{1}{2}$ teaspoon
Sesame oil	2 tablespoons
Pepper	$\frac{1}{5}$ teaspoon

Wrapping
Flour	12 cups
Boiling water	4 ozs.
Cold water	3 ozs.
Flour, for drying hands	$\frac{1}{2}$ cup

PROCEDURE

1. Chop pork, add the above seasoning and mix well with chives.
2. Add flour in bowl, then boiling water and cold water, knead into a smooth dough, let stand for 10 minutes, roll and make into oval shape 4″ × 2″.
3. Add one portion of stuffing to wrapping and fold in half, and seal edges by pinching tight.
4. Heat 4 tablespoons oil in pan. Line pan with dumpling, flat side downwards, fry 1 minute until golden brown, then turn and brown by adding a little oil. It is ready to serve when crisp.

To Serve: Dip in red vinegar and shredded root ginger. Makes 20 fried meat dumplings.

Servings: Four to Five

CHICKEN SPRING ROLL

雞絲春卷

Ingredients
Chicken fillet, shredded	10 ozs.
Onions, shredded	4 ozs.
Chives or spring onion, chopped	2 ozs.
Mushroom, soaked and shredded	2 ozs.
*Spring roll wrapping	20 pieces

Seasoning
(for chicken)
Light soy sauce	1 tablespoon
Cornstarch	1 teaspoon
Sesame oil	$\frac{1}{4}$ teaspoon
Sugar	$\frac{1}{4}$ teaspoon
Salt	$\frac{1}{2}$ teaspoon
Oil	1 tablespoon
Water	1 tablespoon
Pepper	$\frac{1}{4}$ teaspoon

(for mushroom)
Wine	1 tablespoon
Sugar	$\frac{1}{2}$ teaspoon

PROCEDURE

1. Season shredded chicken and mushroom and let stand for 10 minutes.
2. Heat 2 tablespoon oil and fry spring onions, chives, chicken and mushrooms. Cool and use as stuffing.
3. Place a small amount of the above mixture on pieces of flour wrapping and make into rolls. Use flour and water mixture to seal.
4. Heat a lot of oil and deep fry chicken spring rolls until crispy.

Servings: Six
*From you Chinese store, or see recipe Page 67.

SWEET WATER CHESTNUT SOUP

鮮馬蹄露

Ingredients

Fresh water chestnut, remove skin, chop	6 ozs.
Water chestnut powder, mix with $\frac{1}{2}$ cup water	6 tablespoons
Water	8 cups
Sugar	7 ozs.
Eggs	2

PROCEDURE

1. Chop water chestnuts into small pieces.

2. Heat 7 cups of boiling water, add sugar and chestnut powder. After boiling, add beaten eggs and then chopped chestnuts. Bring to boil and serve.

Servings: Four

Glossary

Note: Most of the items listed are readily obtainable at Chinese grocers. Where they are not, substitutes have been indicated.

AGAR AGAR Can be obtained in two forms—as a powder or as dried white fibrous strands. Derived from seaweed it is used as a setting agent in Chinese cooking. Easily obtained.

BEAN CURD (Tau Fu) Made from Soy beans and comes in white custard-like squares. Easily obtained.

BLACK BEAN SAUCE To prepare your own, mix well together 4 tablespoons black beans, 2 tablespoons sugar, 2 tablespoons oil. Steam in bowl over boiling water for 3 minutes. Black Bean sauce can be readily obtained already prepared.

CAKE NOODLES One of the many types of noodles, these are bound together in tight balls about the size of a golf ball. Easily obtained.

CHINESE CABBAGE This has white stems and light green tightly bunched leaves. It is a common ingredient in Chinese cooking and is easily obtainable.

CHINESE HAM This may be hard to obtain and local substitutes may have to be used. Chinese ham is preserved in a different way to other ham and it has a distinctive flavour.

CHINESE MUSHROOMS These are dried and smaller than European mushrooms. They have a most distinctive taste and substitutes should not be used. They are readily available at any Chinese grocer.

CHINESE SPOON A spoon made of clay which usually has some Chinese motif painted on it. Chinese spoons are available in different sizes.

CHINESE WINE There are many varieties of Chinese rice wine and dry sherry is usually considered a very suitable substitute for use in cooking.

CHOY SUM A Chinese vegetable which has stems with green leaves. It is fairly easy to obtain.

CLOUD EAR (Wood Ear) (Snow Fungus) (Sea Jelly) (Jelly Sheet) This a dried edible fungus so named for the rather puffy ear shape which it takes on after soaking. It has little flavour and is used mainly to add texture to the food. Cloud Ear is one of several edible wood fungi.

HOI SIN SAUCE A sauce made from Soy beans, sugar, flour, garlic chilli and vinegar. It can be used as a dip for all sorts of meat. Obtainable already prepared at most grocery stores.

LONG BEANS One of the many varieties of Chinese vegetables, long beans are, as their name suggests, longer than ordinary beans. They are obtainable at most Chinese grocers. String beans can be used as a substitute.

MUD Originally "street mud" actually used. Substitute, flour and water made into dough and rolled out to encase Beggar's chicken.

MUSHROOMS (Dried) To prepare for cooking. Soak in boiling water for $\frac{1}{2}$ an hour. Drain, remove stem and season with 1 tablespoon wine and $\frac{1}{2}$ teaspoon sugar.

MUSTARD GREEN Broccoli

O.K. SAUCE If unobtainable at Chinese grocer, prepare by mixing
2 tablespoons Tomato Sauce
1 tablespoon Worstershire Sauce
1 tablespoon Chinese Wine
2 tablespoons Sugar

OLIVE SEED Used for cakes—usually obtainable at Chinese grocers.

CRUSHED PEANUTS Can be used as a substitute.

PLUM SAUCE A sweet and sour sauce made from plums, apricots, vinegar and sugar, chillies and various spices. Easily obtainable.

PRESERVED CHINESE VEGETABLES These are dried vegetables which retain their individual flavour. Usually they are easy to obtain.

ROSE WINE Strong wine which is used mainly in marinades. Use brandy if it is unobtainable.

SEA JELLY Crunchy substance from the sea. Very good for cold plates.

SILVER SPROUTS Snap off head and tail of fresh bean sprouts.

SNOW PEAS These are a delicious winter vegetable, available from your local Chinese greengrocer.

TANG FLOUR This is made from wheat starch and is available at Chinese grocers.

TARO Sweet Potato

TIENTSIN CABBAGE A variety of Chinese cabbage from Tientsin Province. If it is unobtainable Chinese cabbage can be substituted.

WANTON SHEETS These are made from noodle dough (egg and flour) and are usually kept refrigerated until used. Available from Chinese grocers.

Utensils for Chinese Cooking

For successful Chinese cooking it is essential to have
a few simple and inexpensive utensils.

WOK No Chinese chef can be without a Wok. The Wok is simply a shallow pan which permits easy mixing and good heat control. It is probably the most versatile of all cooking pots as just about anything can be prepared in it. It can be used for steaming, stir frying, deep frying, boiling and braising. Woks are very cheap, easy to maintain and durable.

SHOVEL OR SPATULA This is shaped like an egg turner and is an essential companion to the Wok. It usually has a sharp edge for cutting or chopping ingredients in the Wok.

THE CHOPPER The chopper is an essential piece of equipment as a lot of ingredients require very fine chopping. Choppers come in various sizes with the larger cleaver type being used for meat and poultry and the smaller types for vegetables. The correct way to use the chopper is described in the introduction.

CHOPPING BOARD A chopping board should be of a good size and made of wood that is fairly easy to clean.

WIRE SCOOP This is useful for deep frying or boiling as it allows the hot liquid to drain from the food.

LADLES These are useful for serving soup and rice.

CHOPSTICKS Apart from being the utensils which are used to eat the meal, Chopsticks are very handy in the kitchen. They can be used to stir liquids, beat eggs or test meat for tenderness.

STEAMER A metal or bamboo rack steamer capable of holding a good amount of ingredients is most essential.

Fluid

U.K.	U.S.	European
1 teasp.	1¼ teasp.	6.2 millilitres
1 tbsp.	1¼ tbsp.	19 millilitres
3.5 oz.	6⅔ tbsp.	1 decilitre
4 oz.	½ cup (¼ pint)	⅛ litre (approx)
¼ pint	5 oz.	1½ decilitre
8 oz.	1 cup (½ pint)	¼ litre (approx)
½ pint	10 oz.	3 decilitre
16 oz.	1 pint	0.47 litre
1 pint	20 oz.	6 decilitres
32 oz.	1 quart	0.95 litre
34 oz.	4⅓ cups	1 litre
1 quart	40 oz.	1.2 litres
128 oz.	1 gallon	3.8 litres
1 gallon	160 oz.	4.8 litres

NB: UK pint holds 20 oz., US pint 16 oz.

Oven Temperature

Fahrenheit	Centigrade	Mark (Gas mark)	
250-275	130-140	½ - 1	Very cool
300	150	2	Cool
325	170	3	Warm
350	180	4	Moderate
375-400	190-200	5 - 6	Fairly hot
425	220	7	Hot
450-475	230-240	8 - 9	Very hot

Weight

Ounces	Grams
1	28
1.75	50
2	56
3	85
3.5	100
4	113
5	143
16 (1 lb.)	453
2lb. 2oz.	1000 (1 Kilogram)